The Probabilistic Trader

Mastering Probability, Risk, Strategy, and Psychology for Consistent Trading Success

Deepanshu Suman

First Edition, 2025

Copyright

Title: The Probabilistic Trader
Author: Deepanshu Suman

First Edition
ISBN: 978-93-344-3037-0

Acknowledgments

I would like to express my deepest gratitude to everyone who supported me throughout the journey of writing this book and my trading career.

First, I thank my mentors and colleagues who shared their knowledge, insights, and guidance, helping me develop a practical and data-driven approach to trading.

I am profoundly grateful to my family for their patience, encouragement, and unwavering belief in my vision. Their support made this book possible.

Finally, I would like to thank my readers. Your curiosity, dedication, and desire to learn are the reason this book exists. I hope the strategies, exercises, and insights shared here empower you to approach trading with confidence, discipline, and a probabilistic mindset.

Dedication

To all dreamers,

who dare to imagine bigger, reach higher, and turn their ambitions into reality. May this book guide you to trade not just with skill, but with vision and courage.

Why This Book Matters

Trading isn't just about charts, numbers, or strategies. At its core, trading is a journey — one that tests patience, discipline, emotional resilience, and the ability to make decisions under uncertainty. Every trader starts with a dream: to turn insight into profit, to beat the market, to build lasting wealth. Yet, most struggle. Around **90% of traders lose money** in their first years.

So, why read another trading book? Because this isn't just another manual. This book is designed to give you something most traders never truly master: a **probabilistic mindset** — the ability to approach trading as a calculated, disciplined process rather than a gamble.

The Problem Most Traders Face

Many books teach *how* to trade, but few teach *why* trading works and *how to think about it.* Traders often jump between strategies, chasing quick wins without understanding probabilities. This leads to emotional decision-making, overtrading, and burnout.

This book is different. It's built on a foundation of **probability, discipline, and systems thinking** — a framework designed to transform your approach to markets and decision-making. It's not about finding "the holy grail" of trading strategies; it's about building your own edge and consistently stacking the odds in your favor.

What You Will Gain

By reading this book, you will:

- **Learn market mechanics** — not just "how to trade," but the structure behind market movements.

- **Develop a probabilistic mindset** for managing risk and filtering noise.
- **Master strategies** for beginners and advanced traders.
- **Build a personal trading system** suited to your style and risk tolerance.
- **Strengthen your psychology** to handle losses and avoid emotional pitfalls.
- **Prepare for the future of trading**, including AI and global market changes.

Why This Matters Now

Markets today move faster and are more complex than ever. Algorithmic trading, AI, and global connectivity have made the trading landscape both promising and challenging. Without a strong framework, it's easy to feel lost. This book gives you the **tools, mindset, and frameworks** to navigate uncertainty and make consistent progress.

A Personal Invitation

Whether you're a beginner seeking clarity or an experienced trader refining your approach, this book matters because it reframes trading as a **science of probabilities** rather than a pursuit of certainty. Trading is not just about money — it's about mastery: mastering the markets and mastering yourself. This book exists to help you do both.

Contents

Preface

Why I Wrote This Book

Financial markets are full of opportunity, but they are also filled with myths, misconceptions, and emotional traps. Many aspiring traders and investors struggle because they lack a structured approach, a clear understanding of risk, or a mindset that focuses on probabilities rather than hope.

I wrote this book to provide a comprehensive, practical, and probabilistic framework for trading and investing. My goal is to help readers:

- Develop a disciplined, data-driven approach to the markets.
- Understand the mechanics of trading across stocks, forex, crypto, and commodities.
- Build a mindset that prioritizes long-term consistency over short-term luck.
- Apply strategies, exercises, and case studies that reinforce learning and skill development.

This book is designed for both beginners seeking foundational knowledge and experienced traders aiming to refine their process, reduce emotional bias, and improve decision-making in uncertain markets.

My Trading & Investing Journey

My journey in the financial markets began like many others: curious, ambitious, and a bit uncertain. I started by exploring stocks, currencies, and eventually cryptocurrencies, learning firsthand the thrill of gains and the sting of losses.

Over time, I realized that success in trading isn't about luck—it's about preparation, discipline, and understanding probabilities. Each trade taught me lessons about risk, strategy, and human psychology. Mistakes were my greatest teachers, showing me where I needed to refine my approach and mindset.

Through years of practice, research, and reflection, I developed a systematic, probabilistic approach to trading that focuses on controlling risk, analyzing data, and making decisions with an edge. This framework is what I share in this book, aiming to help others shorten the learning curve and trade with confidence.

How to Use This Book (Exercises, Journals, Case Studies)

This book is not just for reading—it's **meant to be used**:

1. **Read, Then Apply:** Each chapter contains examples and exercises. After reading, **practice what you learned** on a demo account or paper trading environment.

2. **Keep a Journal:** Track every trade, decision, and emotion. Use the templates in the appendices to **record your trades systematically**.

3. **Work Through Case Studies:** Each chapter has real-world trade examples. Study them, analyze mistakes, and **apply lessons to your trades**.

4. **Use Checklists:** Checklists ensure you don't skip crucial steps like risk assessment, position sizing, or market research.

5. **Iterate & Improve:** Markets change and so should your strategies. Revisit your journal, review results, and **refine your approach continuously**.

Disclaimer: Risk Awareness

Trading involves **substantial risk**. You can lose part or all of your invested capital. This book is intended for **educational purposes only** and does not constitute financial advice.

Before applying any strategies, consider the following:

- Understand the **risk and reward profile** of every trade.
- Start with **small amounts or demo accounts** until you gain confidence.
- Never trade money you cannot afford to lose.
- Market conditions can change rapidly; stay informed and vigilant.
- Seek professional advice if you are unsure about any strategy or instrument.

By reading this book, you acknowledge that trading carries inherent risks and that **success requires discipline, preparation, practice, and patience**. Treat every trade as a probabilistic decision, not a gamble.

The Probabilistic Mindset: Thinking in Odds

Successful trading is not about guessing the future—it is about evaluating **probabilities** and making decisions based on expected outcomes. A probabilistic mindset allows you to:

- Assess the likelihood of various market scenarios.
- Make informed decisions that balance potential **risk and reward**.
- Accept that losses are part of the process and focus on **expected value** over time.
- Reduce emotional reactions to volatility by relying on data and analysis.

Example: Consider a trade with a 60% chance to gain \$100 and a 40% chance to lose \$50. The expected value (EV) of this trade is:

$$EV = (0.6 \times 100) + (0.4 \times -50) = 60 - 20 = 40$$

This means that, on average, each trade is expected to yield a profit of \$40. While individual outcomes are uncertain, executing such trades consistently over time is statistically profitable.

Part I

Foundations

Chapter 1

Introduction to Financial Markets

Introduction

Financial markets are the beating heart of the global economy where buyers and sellers meet to exchange capital, ideas, and risk. From the stock exchanges of New York and London to the crypto platforms operating 24/7, markets shape everything from government policies to household budgets. Yet, for a newcomer, the sheer variety of markets and participants can feel overwhelming.

This chapter provides a clear roadmap to understanding the essentials: what trading really means, the different kinds of markets you can participate in, and the distinction between retail and institutional players. We'll also look at how global time zones influence trading activity and why market hours matter. Along the way, you'll explore visuals that map the world's major markets and practice exercises that help you track real movements over time.

By the end, you'll not only grasp the structure of financial markets but also develop the observational habits of a thoughtful participant someone who sees beyond the noise to the underlying patterns.

A Story

The First Trade - Ravi (Mumbai)

Meet Ravi, a young engineer in Mumbai. One evening, he reads that Bitcoin prices are soaring. Excited, he downloads a trading app, deposits $150, and buys Bitcoin. Within hours, the price drops 5%. Ravi feels a surge of anxiety—but when the price rebounds the next day, he's hooked.

Ravi's experience mirrors that of many new traders: curiosity, excitement, and often a lack of structure. The thrill of early gains can be intoxicating, but without a solid understanding of market mechanics and trading foundations, that excitement can quickly turn into costly mistakes.

Key takeaway: Combine curiosity with knowledge and discipline to navigate markets successfully.

Swinging the Market - Emily (New York)

Emily, a software analyst in New York, decides to try swing trading after reading about short-term stock trends. She invests $5,000 in a tech stock showing strong momentum. Within two days, the stock rises 8%, and Emily celebrates her quick win.

However, without a proper risk management plan, she later holds onto a losing position, hoping it will bounce back. By the end of the week, she loses a portion of her profits. Emily realizes that even with good timing, trades require structure and planning to protect capital.

Key takeaway: Timing matters, but risk management and position sizing are crucial for sustainable trading.

Crypto Volatility - Liam (London)

Liam, a London-based fintech enthusiast, jumps into Ethereum trading after seeing social media hype. He invests £2,000 and watches the price swing 12% in a single day. The rapid volatility excites him, but also triggers impulsive decisions—he buys more during spikes and sells during dips.

After a week of emotional trading, Liam reviews his trades and notices that his gains were often wiped out by poor exit strategies and overtrading. He decides to adopt a probabilistic approach, combining technical analysis, market structure, and discipline.

Key takeaway: Emotional trading erodes profits; structured strategies and probabilistic thinking lead to consistent results.

1.1 What is Trading?

Trading is the exchange of financial instruments—such as stocks, currencies, cryptocurrencies, commodities, or bonds—for profit. Unlike investing, which focuses on long-term growth, trading seeks to capture opportunities from short- and medium-term price movements.

Trading is both an art and a science. The art comes from understanding market sentiment, reading price action, and interpreting news or events. The science comes from analyzing data, managing risk, and applying structured strategies to make probabilistic decisions.

> *Trading is not predicting the future. It is managing uncertainty in a way that gives you an edge.*

Key Aspects of Trading

Trading requires mastery of several fundamental principles that separate consistent traders from casual participants:

- **Speculation:** Traders aim to profit from anticipated price movements, focusing on short- to medium-term opportunities using patterns, news, and market sentiment.

- **Liquidity:** Liquidity measures how easily an asset can be bought or sold without affecting its price. High liquidity allows smooth entries and exits; low liquidity increases slippage and unpredictability.

- **Risk and Reward:** Every trade carries potential gain and potential loss. Proper risk management—including stop losses, position sizing, and diversification—protects capital while seeking profits.

- **Time Horizons:** Trading ranges from seconds (high-frequency) to months (swing trading). Each horizon demands different strategies, mindset, and risk management.

- **Market Mechanics:** Understanding order types, bid-ask spreads, volume, and market depth is essential for anticipating execution outcomes and minimizing costs.

- **Probability and Decision-Making:** Trading is about managing uncertainty. Probabilistic thinking, structured strategies, and pattern recognition increase the likelihood of consistent success.

- **Discipline and Psychology:** Emotional control is critical. Fear, greed, and impulsive actions can undermine even the best strategies. Journaling trades and following a plan are essential for long-term profitability.

Case in Point

Consider a trader buying a tech stock ahead of a positive earnings report. If the report exceeds expectations, the stock rises and the trader profits. If it misses, the trader loses. The difference lies in preparation, analysis, and probability-based decision-making.

Key Takeaway

Trading is not gambling. It is a disciplined, systematic approach to buying and selling assets where informed, probabilistic decisions enhance the likelihood of consistent profits.

Case Study: Tesla Stock in 2020

In March 2020, Tesla traded at approximately $85 (split-adjusted). By August 2020, it had surged above $400.

Traders who applied momentum strategies, managed risk carefully, and followed structured plans captured extraordinary returns. In contrast, those who entered impulsively or chased hype without preparation often suffered significant losses due to the stock's extreme volatility.

Key takeaway: Even in high-volatility markets, disciplined strategies and probabilistic thinking differentiate successful traders from those driven by emotion or luck.

1.2 Types of Markets: Stocks, Forex, Crypto, Commodities, Bonds

Traders operate across a variety of markets, each with unique characteristics, risk profiles, and opportunities. Understanding these markets is essential for developing effective strategies.

Stocks

Stocks represent ownership in companies and are traded on exchanges like the NYSE, NASDAQ, or NSE. Traders profit from price appreciation and dividends. Stock prices are influenced by company performance, economic conditions, and market sentiment.

Forex (Foreign Exchange)

Forex trading involves currency pairs (e.g., USD/EUR) and is the largest, most liquid market in the world, with over $6 trillion traded daily. Prices are affected by economic indicators, geopolitical events, and central bank policies. Forex trading often requires leverage due to smaller price movements.

Cryptocurrencies

Cryptos like Bitcoin, Ethereum, and others are digital assets traded 24/7. Known for high volatility, they can generate rapid profits but also substantial losses. Factors include adoption trends, regulation, and market sentiment.

Commodities

Commodities include physical goods like gold, oil, and agricultural products. Prices are influenced by supply-demand dynamics, geopolitical events, and global economic trends. Traders can use futures and options to speculate or hedge.

Bonds

Bonds are debt instruments issued by governments or corporations. Traders profit from interest payments and price fluctuations. Bond markets are typically less volatile than stocks or crypto but are sensitive to interest rates and credit risk.

Market	**Average Daily Volume**
Stocks (Global)	$200B
Forex	$6T
Crypto	$50B–$150B
Commodities	$30B
Bonds	$800B

Key takeaway: Each market has distinct behavior, risk levels, and opportunities. Understanding these differences allows traders to tailor strategies effectively and manage risk across multiple asset classes.

1.3 Who Trades? Retail vs Institutional Investors

Markets are composed of a wide range of participants, each with different resources, objectives, and strategies. Understanding who trades and how they operate is essential for any aspiring trader.

Retail Traders

Retail traders are individual investors who trade using personal capital, often through online brokers or trading platforms. They range from beginners exploring their first trades to experienced part-time traders. Key characteristics include:

- Limited capital compared to institutions
- Access to standard trading tools and research
- Greater susceptibility to emotional decisions
- Focus on short- to medium-term trades

Institutional Traders

Institutional traders represent large organizations, such as hedge funds, mutual funds, banks, and pension funds. They trade with significant capital, advanced technology, and access to proprietary research. Key characteristics include:

- Large-scale trades that can influence market prices
- Sophisticated risk management and algorithmic strategies
- Access to detailed market data and analytics
- Long-term investment and hedging strategies

Key Differences and Insights

- Retail traders often react to news and hype, while institutions plan trades based on research and probabilistic models.
- Understanding institutional behavior can help retail traders anticipate market movements.
- Successful trading requires learning from institutional practices—discipline, risk management, and data-driven strategies—while leveraging the agility of retail trading.

Key takeaway: Recognizing the differences between retail and institutional traders helps you navigate markets more strategically, anticipate price movements, and adopt professional-grade trading habits.

1.4 Market Hours, Time Zones, and Where to Trade

Traders operate across multiple markets worldwide. Knowing market hours, time zone differences, and trading venues is essential to capture liquidity, volatility, and opportunities.

Global Stock Markets

- **NYSE/NASDAQ (USA):** 14:30 – 21:00 UTC
- **LSE (UK):** 08:00 – 16:30 UTC
- **Euronext / Frankfurt (EU):** 08:00 – 16:30 UTC
- **TSE (Japan):** 00:00 – 06:00 UTC
- **ASX (Australia):** 23:00 – 05:00 UTC
- **NSE/BSE (India):** 03:45 – 10:00 UTC
- **HKEX (Hong Kong):** 01:30 – 08:00 UTC

Where to trade: Retail traders can use brokers like Interactive Brokers, TD Ameritrade, Saxo Bank, or local exchanges via authorized brokers.

Forex Market

- **Tokyo / Asia Session:** 00:00 – 09:00 UTC
- **London / Europe Session:** 07:00 – 16:00 UTC
- **New York / USA Session:** 12:00 – 21:00 UTC

Where to trade: Popular forex brokers include OANDA, IG, Forex.com, Saxo Bank, and Interactive Brokers or any other regulated forex brokers.

Cryptocurrency Markets

Cryptocurrencies trade **24/7 globally**. Prices can be highly volatile during news events or when traditional markets are closed.

Where to trade: Binance, Coinbase, Kraken, Bitstamp, FTX (regional), and other regulated exchanges.

Commodities

Traded mostly on futures exchanges:

- **CME (USA):** Oil, Gold, Indices — nearly 24 hours with short breaks
- **Tokyo Commodity Exchange (Japan):** Metals, Energy
- **MCX (India):** Gold, Silver, Energy, Agri
- **ICE (UK/Europe):** Oil, Coffee, Sugar

Where to trade: Use regulated futures brokers or platforms that provide access to global commodity exchanges.

Bonds

Bonds trade mostly during regional business hours:

- Government bonds: USA (CME, 14:30 – 21:00 UTC), EU (08:00 – 16:30 UTC)
- Corporate bonds: Exchange or OTC, depending on issuer

Where to trade: Interactive Brokers, Fidelity, Charles Schwab, or local authorized brokers.

Tips for Global Traders

- Use **UTC as a reference** to avoid confusion across time zones.
- Focus on **market overlaps** (e.g., London-New York, Tokyo-London) for higher liquidity.
- Use **time zone converters or trading apps** to plan your sessions.
- Crypto markets allow trading **outside traditional market hours**, but volatility can spike unexpectedly.

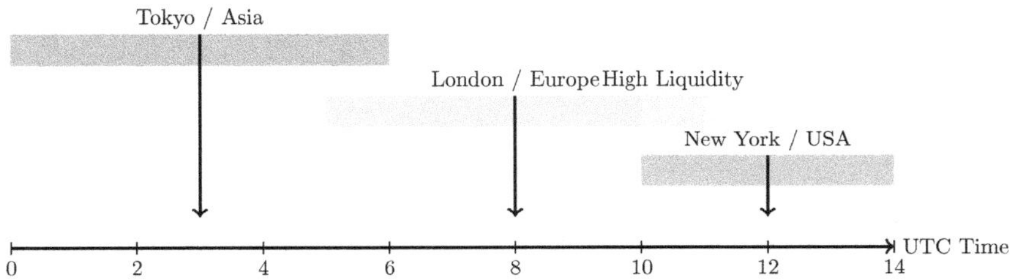

Key takeaway: Understanding global market hours, overlaps, and proper trading venues empowers traders to execute timely, informed trades, regardless of location.

Example: Trading EUR/USD

For currency pairs like EUR/USD, the most active and liquid periods occur during the overlap of the London and New York sessions. This typically happens between 12:00 PM and 4:00 PM UTC. During this window, volatility often spikes, providing better opportunities for entries and exits.

Action Tip: Traders can plan trades around these overlaps to capture larger moves while minimizing slippage. Avoid trading during low-volume periods, such as late Asian session hours, unless using specific strategies designed for low liquidity.

Exercise: Track 3 Markets for a Week

Objective: Observe market behavior, identify active periods, and refine your focus.

1. Select three markets to follow (e.g., a stock like Tesla, a forex pair like EUR/USD, and a cryptocurrency like Bitcoin).

2. Use a demo or paper trading account to monitor price movements without risking real money.
3. Record daily observations in a trading journal:
    - Times when price moves are most significant
    - News or events correlating with market movements
    - Personal comfort and ease in analyzing each market
4. At the end of the week, review your notes to identify patterns, volatility periods, and which market aligns best with your trading style.

Key Takeaways

- Choose a primary market to focus on; mastering one before diversifying increases your chances of success.
- Trading is about observing patterns, volatility, and market behavior — not guessing.
- Use demo or paper trading accounts to practice safely and build confidence.
- Journaling is critical: record market movements, news correlations, session overlaps, and emotional reactions.
- Weekly reviews help identify patterns, refine strategies, and determine which markets suit your trading style.
- Understanding market hours and session overlaps allows you to trade when liquidity and volatility are highest.
- Actionable observation and disciplined practice form the foundation of profitable trading.

Chapter 2

Trading vs. Investing

Introduction

Before diving into market mechanics, it's crucial to understand one of the most fundamental distinctions: the difference between **trading** and **investing**. At first glance, both involve buying assets with the hope that their value rises. But the mindset, strategy, and outcomes are strikingly different.

Investors build wealth gradually, focusing on long-term growth, compounding, and patience. Traders, however, aim to profit from short-term price movements, often using technical analysis, timing, and sometimes leverage.

Knowing where you fit on this spectrum is essential, because your approach will shape your goals, risk tolerance, and day-to-day decisions in the market.

A Story: Two Paths, One Goal

Meet Alex and Priya.

Alex, an aspiring investor, researched companies with strong financials and long-term growth potential. He bought shares in a renewable energy company and held them for years, focusing on dividends and steady appreciation.

Priya, on the other hand, was drawn to trading. She watched daily price charts, identified patterns, and executed trades on momentum. Some days she profited, others she lost, but she kept meticulous records, refined strategies, and treated every trade as a calculated decision.

Both sought wealth, but their paths were different. Alex relied on patience and fundamentals; Priya relied on timing, probability, and disciplined execution.

This chapter will help you understand these approaches, so you can identify whether your style leans toward trading, investing, or a combination of both.

2.1 Differences in Mindset and Time Horizons

When entering financial markets, one of the first distinctions a learner must make is between the **short-term mindset of traders** and the **long-term outlook of investors**. Both approaches seek profit, but they differ in purpose, psychology, and the way time is used as a tool.

The Trader's Mindset

Traders operate with speed and precision. Their focus is on capturing shorter price movements within hours, days, or weeks. This requires:

- Rapid decision-making and adaptability to changing market conditions.
- Emotional discipline to exit both profitable and losing positions quickly.
- Reliance on technical charts, indicators, and patterns to identify opportunities.
- A willingness to accept frequent small losses as part of the process.

In essence, traders think in terms of *probabilities*, not certainties. Each trade is a tactical move, like a chess player making calculated short-term advances. The primary goal is not to predict the far future but to manage risk in the immediate moment.

The Investor's Mindset

Investors adopt a completely different lens. Their focus extends across years or even decades. This perspective emphasizes:

- Patience and resilience through market cycles of boom and bust.
- Confidence in the long-term growth of economies, companies, or asset classes.

- Use of fundamental analysis—earnings, dividends, economic data—over short-term price movements.
- Harnessing the power of compounding returns over extended horizons.

An investor sees daily volatility as "noise" rather than a call to action. The goal is to accumulate assets that appreciate in value or generate cash flow across generations. Warren Buffett's philosophy— *"Our favorite holding period is forever"*—captures this mindset.

The Role of Time Horizons

Time horizon is the invisible thread that separates trading from investing. Consider two individuals:

- A trader buys a stock at $100, aiming to sell at $105 within a week.
- An investor buys the same stock at $100, intending to hold it for ten years, collecting dividends and benefiting from long-term growth.

Both purchase the same asset but play entirely different games. The trader measures success in days or weeks; the investor in years or decades.

Blurring the Lines

It is important to note that the line between trading and investing is not always rigid. Some participants practice **swing trading**, holding positions for weeks, which lies between day trading and long-term investing. Others adopt a **core-and-satellite approach**—investing a large portion for the long term while allocating a smaller portion to active trading.

Key Lesson

Confusion arises when people mix these approaches unconsciously—trading with an investing mindset or investing with a trading mindset. For example, holding onto a losing trade because you suddenly decide to "invest" in it can be dangerous. Clarity on whether you are *trading* or *investing* ensures that your risk management, tools, and expectations align with your chosen path.

Key Takeaways

- Trading is about short-term moves, speed, and probability.

- Investing is about long-term growth, patience, and compounding.
- Time horizon is the central dividing line—days and weeks vs. years and decades.
- Mixing trading and investing without clear boundaries often leads to poor outcomes.
- Choose the mindset that aligns with your goals, personality, and tolerance for risk.

2.2 Short-term vs Long-term Strategies

When approaching financial markets, one of the most practical distinctions is between **short-term trading strategies** and **long-term investing strategies**. While they both involve the same financial instruments—stocks, currencies, or crypto—the way they are applied, the goals they serve, and the risks they carry are very different.

Short-term Strategies (Trading) Short-term strategies are focused on capturing price movements over hours, days, or weeks. Traders often rely on **technical analysis**—charts, indicators, and price patterns—to make decisions.

Common approaches include:

- **Day Trading:** Buying and selling within the same day to capture intraday volatility.
- **Swing Trading:** Holding positions for several days to weeks, aiming to profit from medium-term price trends.
- **Scalping:** Executing dozens or hundreds of small trades to capture tiny price differences.

These methods demand constant monitoring, quick decision-making, and emotional discipline. Short-term trading can generate faster returns but also exposes the trader to higher transaction costs and amplified emotional stress.

Example: A trader might buy EUR/USD at 1.0850 in the London session, aiming to sell at 1.0870 within hours. The profit is small, but the turnover is frequent.

Long-term Strategies (Investing) Long-term strategies are built on holding positions for years or even decades. Investors look at **fundamental analysis**—company earnings, economic growth, industry trends, and valuation metrics—to decide where to allocate their capital.

Common approaches include:

- **Buy and Hold:** Purchasing strong companies or index funds and holding them for long periods regardless of market cycles.
- **Dividend Investing:** Accumulating stocks that generate steady dividend income, reinvested over time.
- **Value and Growth Investing:** Selecting undervalued companies or those with high growth potential and allowing compounding to work over decades.

Long-term investing benefits from lower costs, less emotional strain, and the mathematical power of compounding returns. However, it requires patience and the ability to endure market downturns without panicking.

Example: An investor buys Tesla shares in 2015 and holds them through volatility, reaping exponential gains by 2021.

Blending the Two

Not every market participant falls neatly into one category. Some people invest most of their portfolio for the long term while allocating a smaller amount to short-term trades. This hybrid approach allows them to build wealth steadily while also satisfying the urge to act on short-term opportunities.

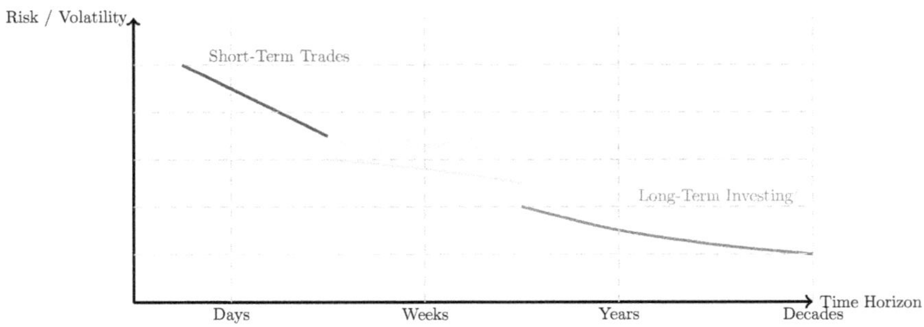

2.3 Case Study: Swing Trade vs Buy-and-Hold

Let's compare two approaches using Bitcoin as an example:

- **Trader (Swing Trade):** Buys Bitcoin at $28,000 and sells at $32,000 within 2 weeks. Profit = 14% before fees.
- **Investor (Buy-and-Hold):** Buys Bitcoin at $28,000 and holds for 3 months. Price moves to $31,000. Profit = 10.7%.

Key Insights

- Short-term strategies prioritize speed, technical analysis, and quick execution.
- Long-term strategies prioritize patience, fundamentals, and compounding.
- Your chosen approach should align with your *time availability, personality, and financial goals.*
- Traders often borrow capital (margin) to increase position size, aiming to amplify gains. But leverage cuts both ways—losses are also magnified.
- Investors usually avoid high leverage, preferring compounding returns and steady growth.

Story: In 2020, a young retail trader in the U.S. used margin to buy call options on a popular stock. Overnight, the stock dropped 15%. With 10x leverage, their account was wiped out in hours. An investor holding the same stock experienced a temporary drawdown, but three years later, that stock had doubled.
Key Difference: The trader realizes profits quickly but needs precise timing and execution. The investor earns slightly less but experiences fewer transactions, less stress, and benefits from long-term compounding.

2.4 Leverage & Margin: Power and Danger

Leverage and margin are fundamental tools in trading that allow you to control a larger position with a relatively small amount of capital. While they can amplify profits, they also magnify losses, making understanding their proper use essential for any trader.

What is Leverage?

Leverage is essentially borrowing money from a broker to increase your exposure to a market. For example, 10:1 leverage means that for every $1 of your own capital, you can control $10 worth of an asset.

What is Margin?

Margin is the collateral you need to maintain your leveraged positions. It acts as a safety buffer for the broker to cover potential losses. There are two main types:

- **Initial Margin:** The amount required to open a position.
- **Maintenance Margin:** The minimum account balance required to keep a position open.

The Power of Leverage

Leverage allows traders to:

- Increase potential returns from small price movements.
- Diversify positions without deploying large amounts of capital.
- Enter markets that may otherwise be inaccessible due to high prices.

The Danger of Leverage

Improper use of leverage can lead to:

- Rapid depletion of your account during adverse moves.
- Margin calls, forcing liquidation at a loss.
- Emotional stress that can impair judgment and discipline.

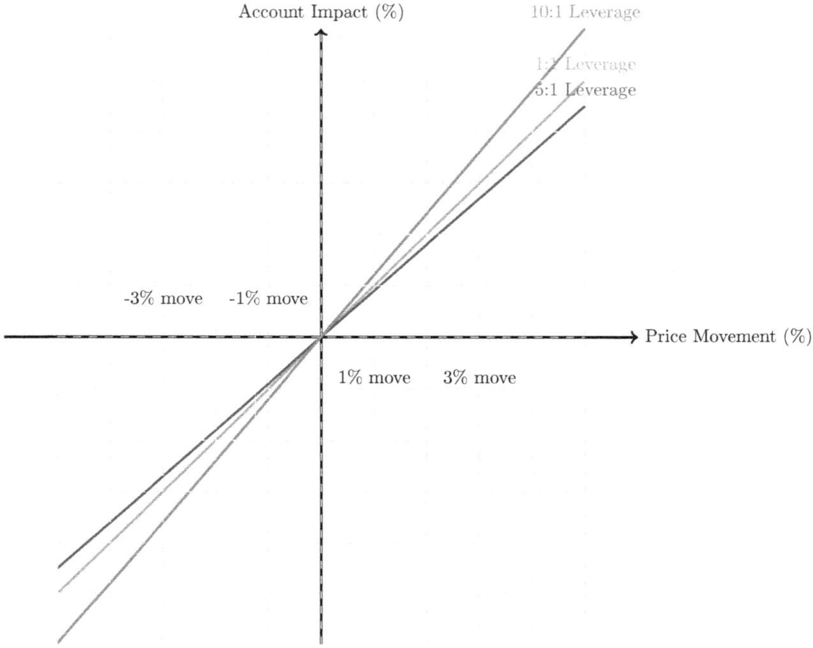

Case Study: EUR/USD Trade

Suppose a trader opens a $10,000 account and uses 50:1 leverage to trade EUR/USD.

- Position Size: $500,000 controlled.
- Price moves 1% against the trader → $5,000 loss (50% of account).
- Price moves 1% in favor → $5,000 profit (50% of account).

This example shows that while leverage can amplify profits, a small adverse move can wipe out a significant portion of capital.

2.5 Time Horizons: Day Traders vs Wealth Builders

Trading strategies vary widely depending on the time horizon a trader adopts. Understanding your time horizon is crucial, as it dictates your approach, risk tolerance, and capital allocation.

Day Traders

Day traders focus on short-term price movements, often opening and closing positions within the same trading day. They aim to profit from intraday volatility rather than long-term trends.

- **Typical Holding Period:** Minutes to hours.
- **Tools Used:** Technical indicators, real-time charts, news feeds.
- **Risk Profile:** High — rapid gains possible but losses accumulate quickly without discipline.

Example: A trader notices a breakout in EUR/USD at 9:30 AM UTC. They enter a position and close it two hours later for a 0.5% profit. Multiple trades like this compound gains across the day.

Swing Traders

Swing traders hold positions for days to weeks, aiming to capture short- to medium-term trends. They often combine technical and fundamental analysis to time entries and exits.

- **Typical Holding Period:** 1–14 days.
- **Tools Used:** Chart patterns, moving averages, earnings reports.
- **Risk Profile:** Moderate — more time to analyze trends but exposed to overnight market moves.

Example: A trader buys Tesla stock anticipating a positive earnings report. They hold for a week until the stock rises 8%, then exit.

Wealth Builders / Long-Term Investors

Wealth builders focus on long-term growth, often holding positions for months or years. Their strategies emphasize portfolio growth, dividends, and compounding rather than short-term volatility.

- **Typical Holding Period:** Months to years.
- **Tools Used:** Fundamental analysis, economic trends, company financials.

- **Risk Profile:** Lower daily volatility but exposed to macroeconomic and market cycles.

Example: An investor buys shares of Apple, holding for 5 years to benefit from product growth, dividends, and stock appreciation.

Action Guidance

1. Identify your preferred trading horizon based on personality, time availability, and capital.
2. Start with one time horizon until you gain mastery, then diversify if desired.
3. Keep a journal tracking duration, entry/exit logic, and outcomes.

Key Takeaways

- Day trading is fast-paced and requires constant attention; suitable for disciplined, short-term-focused traders.
- Swing trading balances short-term opportunities with slightly longer trends; allows more flexibility.
- Long-term investing prioritizes wealth accumulation and is less affected by daily fluctuations.
- Choosing the right horizon aligns your strategy with your goals, risk tolerance, and lifestyle.

Action Guidance

1. Start with low leverage (e.g., 2:1 to 5:1) until you understand its impact.
2. Always calculate potential loss before entering a trade.
3. Use stop-loss orders to manage risk.
4. Never risk more than 1-2% of your capital on a single leveraged trade.

Key Takeaways

- Leverage magnifies both profits and losses; use it responsibly.
- Margin requirements ensure brokers are protected but can trigger rapid liquidation.
- Start small, understand the mechanics, and develop discipline before scaling up.
- Proper risk management is critical when using leverage.

Case Study: Swing Trade vs Buy-and-Hold Over 3 Months

To illustrate the difference between short-term trading and long-term investing, consider the following scenario:

Scenario: An investor has $10,000 and is considering two approaches with a tech stock (e.g., Apple):

- **Buy-and-Hold:** Purchase the stock and hold for 3 months, relying on the company's growth and market trends.
- **Swing Trade:** Use technical analysis to identify short-term price swings, entering and exiting multiple trades within the same 3-month period.

Results:

- **Buy-and-Hold:** Stock rises steadily by 12%. Investor earns $1,200 profit with minimal stress.
- **Swing Trade:** Trader executes 6 successful trades and 2 losses. Net profit is $1,500 but involves constant monitoring, emotional discipline, and transaction costs.

Key Insights:

1. Swing trading can generate higher returns in the short term but requires skill, attention, and risk management.
2. Buy-and-hold provides steady, predictable growth and is suitable for long-term wealth building.
3. Traders must align their strategy with their goals, time availability, and risk tolerance.

Exercise: Choose a stock or crypto asset and simulate a 3-month buy-and-hold versus swing-trade scenario using a demo account. Record profits, losses, and emotional experience to understand which style suits you better.

Checklist: "Am I Trading or Investing?"

Use this decision filter to clarify your approach before entering a trade or investment:

1. **Time Horizon:** Am I looking to hold for minutes/days (trading) or months/years (investing)?

2. **Goal:** Is my objective short-term profit or long-term wealth accumulation?

3. **Research Focus:** Am I analyzing price action, patterns, and market sentiment (trading) or company fundamentals and growth prospects (investing)?

4. **Risk Tolerance:** Can I handle high daily volatility (trading) or prefer steadier, long-term returns (investing)?

5. **Decision Frequency:** Will I make multiple decisions per week/day (trading) or fewer, long-term decisions (investing)?

6. **Emotional Readiness:** Am I prepared for frequent ups and downs or comfortable with slower, steadier changes?

Key Takeaway: Understanding whether you are trading or investing will help you select strategies, manage risk, and avoid confusion that can erode profits.

Key Takeaways

- **Mindset Matters:** Trading and investing require distinct mindsets trading is short-term and active, while investing is long-term and strategic.

- **Time Horizons Define Strategy:** Short-term traders focus on minutes to weeks, while investors look at months to years.

- **Leverage is a Double-Edged Sword:** It can magnify gains but also increase losses; understanding margin requirements is crucial.

- **Risk Profiles Differ:** Trading involves higher volatility and frequent decision-making; investing prioritizes steady growth and compounding.
- **Allocation Can Be Hybrid:** Many professionals combine strategies, e.g., allocating part of capital to trading and part to long-term investing.
- **Decision Framework Helps:** Use checklists and journaling to clarify whether a move is trading or investing, reducing emotional mistakes.
- **Practice and Observation:** Simulating trades and tracking long-term positions builds skill, discipline, and understanding of market behavior.

Chapter 3

Understanding Market Mechanics

Introduction

Before you can trade effectively, it's essential to understand how markets operate behind the scenes. Market mechanics govern the execution of trades, pricing, liquidity, and how orders are matched between buyers and sellers. Without this knowledge, even a well-researched trade can go wrong due to slippage, delayed execution, or unexpected costs.

A Story: Placing the First Trade

Meet Aisha, a young trader exploring the stock market. She's excited to buy Tesla shares but hesitates — should she simply click "Buy" or set a limit order? How can she be sure she gets a fair price?

This uncertainty is common for beginners. Market mechanics — the rules and processes behind how trades are executed — determine price, speed, and order fulfillment. By understanding these mechanics, traders like Aisha can navigate the market confidently, avoid costly mistakes, and implement strategies with precision.

3.1 Order Types: Market, Limit, Stop, Stop-Limit

Placing an order in a market might seem simple — click "buy" or "sell" — but the type of order you choose can significantly impact your profit, risk, and execution. Understanding order types is essential for every trader.

Market Orders

A market order is executed immediately at the best available price. Speed is prioritized over price.

> *Example: Aisha wants to buy 10 Tesla shares now. She places a market order and gets the current market price, even if it fluctuates slightly.*

Pros: Immediate execution.
Cons: Possible price slippage in volatile markets.

Limit Orders

A limit order executes only at a specified price or better, giving you control over the entry or exit price.

> *Example: Aisha wants to buy Tesla at $700. She sets a limit order, which executes only if the price drops to $700 or below.*

Pros: Control over price.
Cons: May not execute if the market never reaches the limit.

Stop Orders (Stop-Loss)

Stop orders trigger a market order once a specified price is reached, often used to limit losses.

> *Example: Aisha bought Tesla at $720 and places a stop-loss at $650 to protect herself from large losses.*

Pros: Protects capital automatically.
Cons: Market gaps may lead to execution at a worse price than expected.

Stop-Limit Orders

Stop-limit orders combine the features of stop and limit orders. When the stop price is hit, a limit order is placed rather than a market order.

> *Example: Aisha sets a stop at $650 with a limit of $645. If Tesla falls to $650, a limit order to sell at $645 activates, preventing excessive slippage.*

Pros: Precise control over price.
Cons: May not execute if the limit price is not met.

Key Takeaway: Mastery of order types allows traders to balance speed, price control, and risk. Choosing the right order for the situation is a hallmark of disciplined trading.

3.2 Bid, Ask, and Spread Explained

Every trade involves two prices: the **bid** and the **ask**. Understanding these is fundamental to knowing how much you pay or receive when entering or exiting a trade.

Bid Price

The bid is the highest price a buyer is willing to pay for an asset.

> *Example: If the bid for Tesla stock is $720, a buyer is ready to purchase shares at that price.*

Ask Price

The ask (or offer) is the lowest price a seller is willing to accept.

> *Example: If the ask for Tesla is $722, a seller is willing to sell at that price or higher.*

Spread

The **spread** is the difference between the ask and bid price.

$$Spread = Ask - Bid$$

Example: Bid = $720, Ask = $722, Spread = $2. This is the cost of immediately executing a trade.

Spreads vary by market, asset liquidity, and volatility. Tighter spreads are generally better for traders.

Why It Matters

- Determines **entry/exit costs**.
- Impacts profitability for short-term traders.
- Helps identify **market liquidity**: narrower spreads indicate a more liquid market.

Key Takeaway: The bid-ask spread is the "hidden cost" of trading. Mastering it allows traders to optimize timing, minimize costs, and understand market depth.

3.3 Liquidity and Volume Importance

Liquidity and volume are the lifeblood of markets. They determine how easily you can enter or exit trades, the stability of prices, and the overall risk of your positions.

Liquidity

Liquidity is the ease with which an asset can be bought or sold without causing a significant price change. Highly liquid markets allow traders to execute large orders with minimal slippage.

Example: The EUR/USD forex pair is extremely liquid. A trader can buy or sell millions of dollars without dramatically moving the price. Conversely, a small-cap stock may have low liquidity, making it hard to sell quickly without impacting the price.

Volume

Volume represents the number of shares, contracts, or units traded in a given period. It is a measure of market activity and interest in a particular asset.

Example: Bitcoin's trading volume can spike during major news events. High volume often confirms trends, while low volume can signal uncertainty or potential reversals.

Why It Matters

- High liquidity reduces slippage and trading costs.
- Volume can validate price movements — strong moves with high volume are more reliable.
- Low liquidity or volume increases the risk of unexpected price swings.

Key Takeaway: Understanding liquidity and volume helps traders gauge market health, execute orders efficiently, and avoid costly mistakes during volatile periods.

Why It Matters

- High liquidity reduces slippage and trading costs.
- Volume can validate price movements — strong moves with high volume are more reliable.
- Low liquidity or volume increases the risk of unexpected price swings.

Key Takeaway: Understanding liquidity and volume helps traders gauge market health, execute orders efficiently, and avoid costly mistakes during volatile periods.

3.4 How Exchanges and Brokers Work

Exchanges and brokers are intermediaries that match buyers and sellers in financial markets. Understanding their operation is essential for executing trades efficiently and managing risk.

Understanding the Vertical Order Book

The vertical order book visualizes all active buy and sell orders for a financial instrument. Key components include:

- **Sell Orders (Asks):** Displayed at the top in red blocks. These represent prices where traders are willing to sell. Larger blocks indicate higher order sizes.
- **Buy Orders (Bids):** Displayed at the bottom in green blocks. These are prices where traders are willing to buy. The width of the blocks shows the size of each order.
- **Current Price:** A dashed line in the middle shows the last executed price.
- **Market Orders:** Arrows indicate how market buys "consume" asks from top down, while market sells hit bids from bottom up.

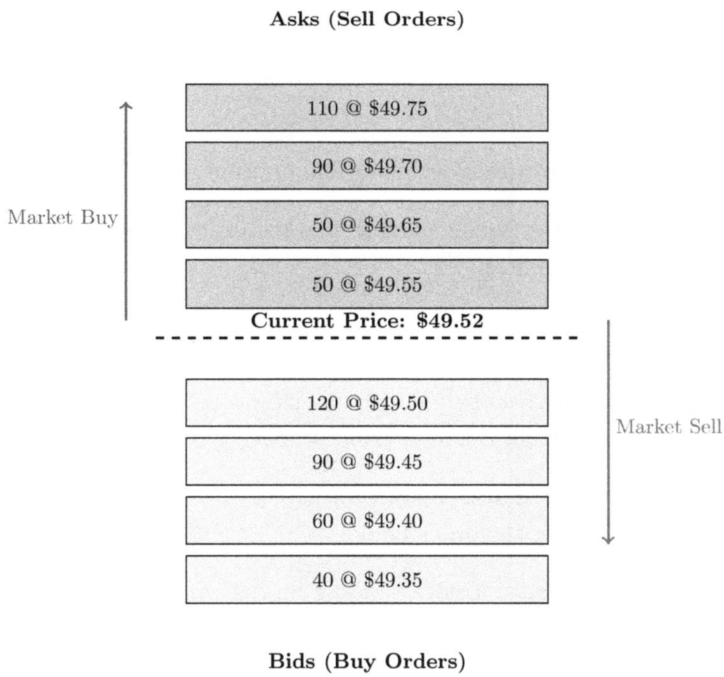

How to Read the Order Book

- **Asks:** Prices sellers are asking. Large orders can indicate resistance.
- **Bids:** Prices buyers are offering. Large bids can indicate support.
- **Current Price:** Shows where the last trade occurred relative to open orders.

- **Market Orders:** Market buys consume ask levels; market sells consume bid levels. The average price may differ from the top ask/bid depending on order size.

Example

Buying 100 units at market price:

- 50 units fill at $49.55 (first ask level)
- 50 units fill at $49.65 (next ask level)

Average purchase price lies at $49.60

Key Takeaways

- Understanding the vertical order book gives traders insight into supply and demand.
- Helps anticipate price movements and plan entries/exits more efficiently.
- Reduces surprises when placing market orders, improving execution and risk management.

Key Insights

1. **Liquidity Awareness:** Wider blocks indicate more liquidity, which means less slippage when entering or exiting trades.
2. **Price Impact:** Large market orders move the price by consuming multiple levels in the order book.
3. **Trading Strategy:** Understanding how the book works allows better timing of entries and exits, and helps in setting realistic stop-loss and take-profit levels.

Exercise

1. Open a demo trading account with any broker that provides an order book view.
2. Observe the depth of bids and asks for a chosen stock, forex pair, or crypto.

3. Place simulated market and limit orders to see how they interact with the order book.

4. Record observations in your trading journal.

Key Takeaways

- Understanding **order types** (Market, Limit, Stop, Stop-Limit) is essential for precise trade execution.
- The **bid, ask, and spread** define the cost of entering and exiting positions and indicate market liquidity.
- **Liquidity and volume** determine how easily trades can be executed and how much impact large orders have on price.
- Exchanges and brokers serve as intermediaries that match buyers and sellers, with the **order book** providing real-time market insight.
- Observing the vertical order book helps traders anticipate price movement, understand supply and demand, and plan entries/exits more effectively.
- Practicing on a demo platform reinforces understanding and prepares you for live trading without risking capital.

Part II

Trading Tools & Techniques

Chapter 4

Technical Analysis

Introduction

Technical analysis is the study of historical price action to forecast future market movements. Unlike fundamental analysis, which examines financial statements, economic indicators, and news events, technical analysis focuses on patterns, trends, and market sentiment reflected in charts.

By learning to read charts, identify trends, and apply indicators, traders gain insights into the probabilities of price movements. This chapter will guide you through the essential tools and techniques for interpreting charts, spotting opportunities, and managing risk effectively.

A Story: Learning to Read the Market

Rohan, a novice trader, opened his first chart and was overwhelmed by candles, lines, and colors. He didn't know which way the price might move. Over time, he learned that charts tell a story — not a guarantee — about market psychology and probable movements. Technical analysis is the trader's lens to interpret price behavior.

4.1 Reading Charts: Line, Bar, Candlestick

Charts are the trader's primary language. Prices are recorded over time, and how we visualize them shapes our ability to spot trends, patterns, and opportunities. The three most common ways to display price data are: **Line**

Charts, **Bar Charts**, and **Candlestick Charts**. Each type provides a different level of detail, moving from the simplest (line) to the most information-rich (candlestick).

Line Charts

A line chart connects the closing prices of a security over time with a simple line.

- **Advantages:** Clean, easy to read, great for identifying broad trends and long-term movement.
- **Limitations:** Ignores intraday detail (open, high, low) — only closing prices are shown.
- **Usage:** Popular among investors tracking overall direction or comparing multiple assets.

Example: A line chart of the NIFTY index over five years clearly shows bull and bear cycles without distracting short-term noise.

Bar Charts (OHLC Charts)

A bar chart (also called OHLC — Open, High, Low, Close) shows more detail than a line chart. Each period is represented by a vertical bar:

- Top of bar = highest price in that period (High).
- Bottom of bar = lowest price in that period (Low).
- Small horizontal tick on the left = opening price (Open).
- Small horizontal tick on the right = closing price (Close).

Interpretation:

- A close higher than the open often signals buying pressure.
- A close lower than the open indicates selling pressure.
- Long bars reflect volatility; short bars show consolidation.

Bar charts balance clarity with detail, making them useful for both trend analysis and intraday study.

Candlestick Charts

Candlesticks are the most popular charting method among traders because they combine detail with visual intuition. Each candlestick represents a specific time period (minute, hour, day, week):

- **Body:** The rectangle formed between open and close.
  - Filled (red/black) = price closed lower than it opened.
  - Hollow (green/white) = price closed higher than it opened.
- **Wicks (Shadows):** Thin lines above and below the body showing the high and low.
- **Open/Close:** The body edges reflect where the price started and ended in that period.

Why Candlesticks Matter:

- They provide immediate insight into market psychology (who's in control — buyers or sellers).
- Patterns formed by one or multiple candles often hint at reversals, continuations, or indecision.
- Easier to read than bar charts because color and shape highlight sentiment.

Comparing the Three

- **Line Chart:** Best for simplicity and trend-tracking.
- **Bar Chart:** Offers complete OHLC detail, more precise than line charts.
- **Candlestick Chart:** Provides the same OHLC detail as bar charts but adds visual clarity and pattern recognition.

Practical Tip: New traders should start with line charts to grasp big-picture movements, then progress to candlesticks for deeper pattern analysis. Bar charts are helpful but less commonly used today due to candlesticks' popularity.

Key Takeaway: Charts are not about predicting the future with certainty, but about organizing price data to reveal probabilities and market behavior. Understanding line, bar, and candlestick charts lays the foundation for technical analysis — turning raw numbers into meaningful stories of market psychology.

4.2 Candlestick Patterns — Types and Interpretation

Candlesticks encode OHLC into compact shapes that reveal market psychology. Traders classify patterns by how many candles they involve and by their typical meaning: reversal, continuation, or indecision. Use patterns as probabilistic signals (not certainties) and always seek confirmation (volume, support/resistance, trend).

Single-Candle Patterns

Hammer

Appearance: Small body near the top, long lower wick.
Psychology: Sellers pushed price down but buyers recovered — possible bullish reversal after a downtrend.
Tip: Wait for confirmation (next candle closes higher).
Reliability: Medium.

Hanging Man

Appearance: Like a hammer but occurs after an uptrend.
Psychology: Warning that sellers tested lower prices — possible bearish reversal.
Tip: Confirm with next bearish candle and rising volume.
Reliability: Medium–Low.

Inverted Hammer / Shooting Star

Appearance: Small body near bottom, long upper wick. Inverted Hammer (after downtrend — bullish hint); Shooting Star (after uptrend — bearish hint).
Tip: Require confirmation; watch for rejection at wick extremes.
Reliability: Medium.

Doji (including Dragonfly and Gravestone)

Appearance: Open and close near equal (very small body); wicks vary.

Dragonfly: long lower wick, no/short upper wick. Gravestone: long upper wick, no/short lower wick.
Psychology: Indecision — potential reversal if appearing at supports / resistances.
Tip: Use with context (trend + support/resistance).
Reliability: Low–Medium.

Spinning Top

Appearance: Small body with upper and lower wicks.
Psychology: Uncertainty; momentum may be weakening.
Reliability: Low.

Marubozu

Appearance: Long body, little or no wicks (bullish or bearish).
Psychology: Strong conviction by buyers (white/green) or sellers (black/red).
Reliability: High (in trend confirmation).

Two-Candle Patterns

Bullish Engulfing

Appearance: Small bearish candle followed by a larger bullish candle that completely engulfs it.
Psychology: Buyers overwhelmed sellers — bullish reversal signal, esp. after downtrend.
Tip: Stronger if engulfing on higher volume.
Reliability: High (with trend/context).

Bearish Engulfing

Opposite of Bullish Engulfing; indicates bearish reversal after an uptrend.

Piercing Pattern

Appearance: Bearish candle followed by bullish candle that closes above mid-point of prior candle.
Psychology: Early bullish reversal sign.
Reliability: Medium.

Dark Cloud Cover

Appearance: Bullish candle followed by bearish candle that closes below mid-point of prior candle.

Psychology: Early bearish reversal sign.
Reliability: Medium.

Harami / Harami Cross

Appearance: Large candle followed by a smaller candle contained within the previous body's range (Harami Cross if second is a Doji).
Psychology: Pausing of prior momentum; potential reversal.
Reliability: Medium–Low.

Tweezer Tops / Tweezer Bottoms

Appearance: Two candles with equal highs (tweezer top) or equal lows (tweezer bottom).
Psychology: Rejection at same price level — possible short-term reversal.
Reliability: Low–Medium.

Three-Candle Patterns

Morning Star

Appearance: Large bearish candle, small-bodied candle (gap down), then large bullish candle that closes into the first candle's body.
Psychology: Strong bullish reversal after a downtrend.
Reliability: High (with confirmation).

Evening Star

Opposite of Morning Star; signals bearish reversal after uptrend.

Three White Soldiers

Appearance: Three consecutive long bullish candles with small wicks opening within previous bodies.
Psychology: Strong bullish continuation/reversal; momentum confirmed.
Reliability: High.

Three Black Crows

Opposite of Three White Soldiers; strong bearish signal.

Three Inside Up / Down

Appearance: A bearish candle, then an inside bullish candle, then a bullish candle closing above the first candle's open (three inside up). Reverse for down.
Reliability: Medium–High.

Continuation Patterns (Multi-Candle)

Rising Three Methods

Appearance: Long bullish candle, small-bodied pullback candles contained within the first candle, then another bullish candle.
Psychology: Temporary profit-taking within an overall bullish trend → continuation.
Reliability: Medium–High.

Falling Three Methods

Opposite; signals continuation of a downtrend.

Tasuki Gaps (Upside / Downside)

Appearance: A gap in trend direction followed by a candle that partially fills the gap but does not close it — continuation sign.
Reliability: Medium.

Other Notable Patterns

Kicker Pattern

Appearance: Sharp opposite-gap open after prior candle (no overlap).
Psychology: Very strong sentiment shift (news-driven).
Reliability: High (but rare; often news-driven).

Doji Combinations / Complex Formations

Various multi-candle doji-based patterns indicate high indecision and require confirmation.

Practical Notes (How to Use Patterns)

- **Context is everything:** Pattern at major support/resistance, trendline, or volume spike is far more meaningful.
- **Confirmations:** Seek confirmation (next candle direction, volume, indicator alignment) before acting.
- **Timeframe matters:** A pattern on a daily chart is more significant than the same pattern on a 5-minute chart.
- **Reliability ranking:** Single-candle signals are weaker than engulfing/three-candle patterns; multi-candle patterns with volume confirmation are strongest.

- **Combine with risk management:** Always define stop-loss and position size — patterns are probabilistic setups, not guarantees.

Key Takeaway: Candlestick patterns translate market psychology into repeatable, probabilistic signals. Learn to recognize them, always use context and confirmation, and treat them as one tool in a larger probabilistic trading process.

4.3 Chart Patterns: Head & Shoulders, Flags, Double Tops

Chart patterns are visual formations on price charts that reflect the psychology of market participants. They occur repeatedly because human behavior — fear, greed, indecision — is consistent across time. By recognizing these patterns, traders can anticipate potential breakouts, reversals, or continuations.

This section covers three of the most widely studied patterns: **Head & Shoulders**, **Flags**, and **Double Tops**.

Head & Shoulders

The **Head & Shoulders** is a reversal pattern that often signals the end of a bullish trend.

- **Formation:**
  - Left Shoulder: Price rises, then pulls back.
  - Head: Price makes a higher peak, then falls again.
  - Right Shoulder: Price rises once more, but forms a lower high.
  - Neckline: The line connecting the two pullback lows.
- **Interpretation:** A break below the neckline after the right shoulder indicates a trend reversal from bullish to bearish.
- **Inverse Version:** The *Inverse Head & Shoulders* signals reversal from bearish to bullish.
- **Practical Tip:** Wait for a confirmed break of the neckline (with volume) before entering trades.

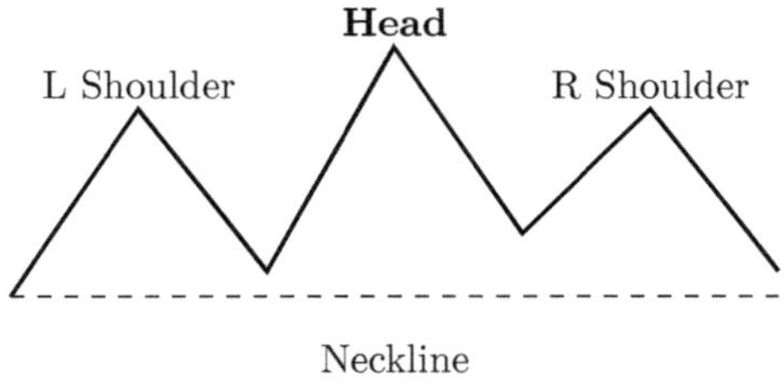

Flags

The **Flag** is a continuation pattern that occurs after a strong price move.

- **Formation:**
  - Flagpole: A sharp, nearly vertical move up or down.
  - Flag: A brief consolidation in a rectangular, sloping channel.
- **Interpretation:** Flags usually resolve in the direction of the preceding trend (uptrend flags break upward, downtrend flags break downward).
- **Types:**
  - Bullish Flag: After a strong upward move, consolidation tilts slightly downward.
  - Bearish Flag: After a sharp downward move, consolidation tilts slightly upward.
- **Practical Tip:** Flags are short-term pauses; the breakout typically matches the length of the flagpole.

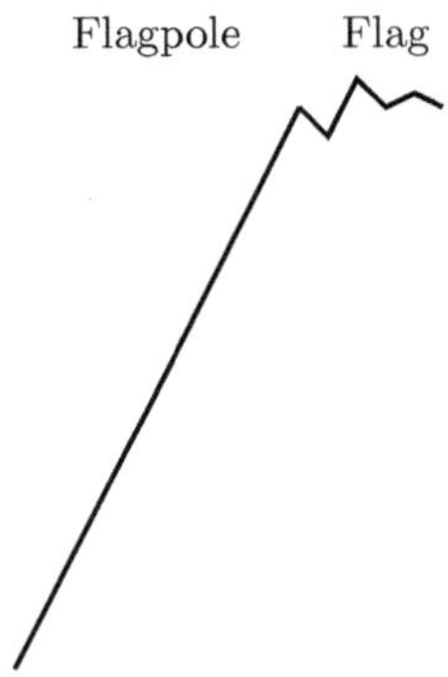

Double Tops

The **Double Top** is another classic reversal pattern that warns of bullish exhaustion.

- **Formation:**
  - Price climbs to a peak, then retraces.
  - Price rises again to roughly the same level, but fails to break higher.
  - The "neckline" is formed at the intermediate low between the two peaks.
- **Interpretation:** A break below the neckline confirms the pattern, often leading to a downward move.
- **Double Bottom:** The opposite pattern signals reversal from bearish to bullish.
- **Practical Tip:** Volume should decline on the second top; if volume is higher, the pattern may fail.

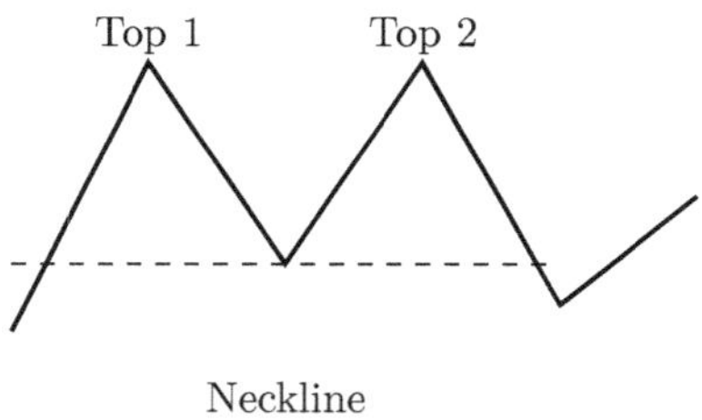

Why These Patterns Matter

- They reflect crowd psychology — greed driving rallies, fear driving sell-offs, hesitation forming consolidations.
- They provide **reference points**: entry triggers (break of neckline or flag), stop-loss placements (above/below pattern), and profit targets (measured move of prior swing).
- No pattern is 100% reliable — confirmation and risk management are crucial.

Key Takeaways

- **Head & Shoulders:** Signals reversal after an uptrend (inverse version works after downtrends).
- **Flags:** Pause-and-go continuation patterns aligned with the main trend.
- **Double Tops/Bottoms:** Classic reversal signals showing trend exhaustion.

Example Exercise: Open a daily chart of a stock (e.g., Apple, Tesla, or Reliance). Try to identify at least one of each pattern in the past 12 months. Mark the neckline or flag boundary and journal how price behaved after the breakout.

4.4 Trend Lines, Support & Resistance

Understanding trend lines, support, and resistance is crucial for interpreting market structure and planning trades. These tools help traders identify potential entry and exit points and the overall market direction.

Trend Lines

A trend line is a straight line that connects two or more price points, providing a visual representation of the market's direction.

- **Uptrend Line:** Connects higher lows in an ascending market. Acts as support.
- **Downtrend Line:** Connects lower highs in a descending market. Acts as resistance.
- **Usage:** Trend lines help identify the prevailing trend and potential reversal points. Breaking a trend line may signal a trend change.

Support and Resistance

- **Support:** A price level where buying interest is strong enough to prevent the price from falling further. Often coincides with previous lows.
- **Resistance:** A price level where selling interest is strong enough to prevent the price from rising further. Often coincides with previous highs.

- **Trading the Levels:** Prices often bounce between support and resistance. Breakouts above resistance or below support can indicate strong momentum.

Examples

- **Uptrend Example:** A stock forms higher lows at $50, $52, $55. Drawing a line through these points shows an uptrend line acting as dynamic support.
- **Resistance Example:** A stock repeatedly fails to rise above $60. Traders may place sell orders near this level until a breakout occurs.

Case Study: Predicting a Breakout in Tesla Stock

In May 2020, Tesla stock was consolidating between $700 and $780 after a strong uptrend. Traders were watching for a breakout that could indicate continuation of the bullish trend.

Step 1: Identify Key Levels

- **Resistance:** $780 — the stock repeatedly failed to rise above this level.
- **Support:** $700 — buyers stepped in to prevent further decline.

Step 2: Draw Trend Lines

- Uptrend line connecting higher lows indicated continued bullish momentum.
- Price compression suggested that volatility was decreasing and a breakout could occur soon.

Step 3: Monitor Volume

- Volume was gradually decreasing during the consolidation phase — typical before a breakout.
- Traders anticipated a surge in volume to confirm a breakout.

Step 4: Prepare for Breakout

- Entry strategy: Place a buy order slightly above $780.
- Stop-loss: Below $770 to limit downside in case of a false breakout.

- Target: Projected based on previous price swings, around $850–$900.

Outcome: Tesla broke above $780 with high volume within a few days, hitting $860. Traders who anticipated the breakout using technical analysis captured significant gains, while those waiting for confirmation missed part of the move.

Key Takeaways:

- Breakouts occur when price consolidates near support/resistance levels.
- Trend lines and volume analysis help anticipate potential moves.
- Predefined entry, stop-loss, and target levels reduce emotional decision-making and manage risk.

Exercise: Identify Patterns on Historical Charts

Objective: Practice spotting chart patterns, such as Head & Shoulders, Flags, and Double Tops, on historical price charts to improve your pattern recognition skills.

Instructions:

1. Select 3–5 historical charts from stocks, forex pairs, or cryptocurrencies.
2. Look for patterns you have learned:
    - Head & Shoulders (reversal patterns)
    - Flags and Pennants (continuation patterns)
    - Double Tops/Bottoms (reversal signals)
3. Mark the support and resistance levels associated with each pattern.
4. Note the breakout or breakdown points and the subsequent price movement.
5. Compare your observations with actual historical outcomes to assess accuracy.

Tips:

- Use different timeframes (daily, 4-hour, 1-hour) to see how patterns appear across scales.
- Focus on volume — breakouts accompanied by high volume are usually more reliable.

- Maintain a trading journal to track your observations, mistakes, and insights.

Outcome: By repeatedly identifying patterns on historical charts, you will build confidence and intuition to recognize them in live markets, improving your technical analysis skills.

Key Takeaways

- **Charts Tell a Story:** Price charts visualize market psychology and past behavior, helping traders anticipate potential moves.
- **Chart Types Matter:** Line charts show overall trends, bar charts display open-high-low-close (OHLC) data, and candlestick charts provide detailed price action insights.
- **Candlestick Patterns:** Patterns like Doji, Hammer, Shooting Star, and Engulfing signal potential reversals or continuations when analyzed in context.
- **Common Chart Patterns:** Head & Shoulders, Flags/Pennants, and Double Tops/Bottoms indicate likely market direction and breakout points.
- **Trend Lines, Support, and Resistance:** Identifying key levels and trend lines helps define entry, exit, and stop-loss points.
- **Volume Confirms Moves:** Rising volume on breakouts or reversals strengthens the reliability of patterns.
- **Practice Improves Accuracy:** Repeatedly identifying patterns on historical charts develops recognition skills and trading intuition.
- **Patterns Are Probabilities, Not Certainties:** Technical analysis provides an edge but does not guarantee outcomes; always manage risk.
- **Journaling Reinforces Learning:** Keeping detailed notes on identified patterns, trades, and outcomes builds long-term skill and discipline.

Chapter 5

Indicators & Oscillators

Introduction

Technical indicators and oscillators are essential tools for traders looking to quantify market behavior. Unlike pure chart patterns, these tools apply mathematical calculations to price and volume data, helping identify trends, momentum, overbought or oversold conditions, and potential reversals.

Understanding indicators allows traders to make probabilistic decisions, complementing their chart-reading skills and improving timing for entries and exits. In this chapter, we explore key indicators, how to interpret them, and how to combine them effectively without overloading your analysis.

A Story: Reading the Signals

Neha, a beginner trader, often felt lost looking at charts. She noticed that prices sometimes bounced predictably, but she couldn't explain why. Then she discovered **technical indicators** — mathematical tools derived from price and volume — which gave her clues about momentum, trend strength, and potential reversals.

5.1 Moving Averages (SMA, EMA)

Moving averages are among the most widely used tools in technical analysis. They smooth out price data over a period to help traders identify trends, filter noise, and generate actionable signals.

Simple Moving Average (SMA)

The Simple Moving Average (SMA) calculates the arithmetic mean of prices over a given period.

$$SMA = \frac{P_1 + P_2 + \ldots + P_n}{n}$$

Example: If a stock closes at \$100, \$102, \$101, \$103, and \$104 over the last 5 days, the 5-day SMA is:

$$SMA = \frac{100 + 102 + 101 + 103 + 104}{5} = 102$$

Uses of SMA:

- **Trend identification:** Rising SMA = uptrend, Falling SMA = downtrend.
- **Support & resistance:** Prices often "bounce" near SMA levels.
- **Crossover signals:** Short-term SMA crossing above long-term SMA = bullish signal (Golden Cross); crossing below = bearish (Death Cross).

Exponential Moving Average (EMA)

EMA gives more weight to recent prices, making it more sensitive to current market changes.

$$EMA_t = \alpha \cdot P_t + (1 - \alpha) \cdot EMA_{t-1}$$

Where $\alpha = \frac{2}{n+1}$ and P_t is the latest price.

Example: For a 10-day EMA, recent prices influence the average more than older prices. This allows traders to react faster to market changes.

Uses of EMA:

- Capturing trends earlier than SMA in volatile markets.
- Generating entry/exit signals via EMA crossovers.
- Combining with indicators like RSI or MACD for stronger confirmation.

Practical Example

Consider a stock where:

- 20-day SMA = \$100
- 50-day SMA = \$98

Since the short-term SMA (20-day) is above the long-term SMA (50-day), it indicates a bullish trend. A trader might consider entering long positions, with stops slightly below recent lows.

Key Takeaways

- SMA smooths price data and is slower to react, useful for long-term trend analysis.
- EMA reacts faster to recent price changes, suitable for short-term and volatile markets.
- Crossovers between SMA/EMA provide actionable trade signals.
- Combining moving averages with other indicators improves trade probability.
- Using multiple timeframes helps traders align short-term and long-term trends.

5.2 RSI, MACD, Bollinger Bands

Technical indicators help traders quantify market momentum, trend strength, and volatility. This section covers three popular indicators used across all markets.

Relative Strength Index (RSI)

RSI measures the speed and change of price movements, oscillating between 0 and 100.

$$RSI = 100 - \frac{100}{1 + RS}, \quad RS = \frac{AverageGain}{AverageLoss}$$

Interpretation:

- RSI >70: Overbought — potential reversal downwards.
- RSI below 30: Oversold — potential reversal upwards.
- Divergence: When price makes a new high but RSI does not, it signals weakening momentum.

Example: A stock is trading at \$50, RSI = 75. The asset may be overbought; cautious traders might wait for a pullback or tighten stop-loss orders.

Moving Average Convergence Divergence (MACD)

MACD shows the relationship between two EMAs (usually 12-day and 26-day).

$$MACD = EMA_{12} - EMA_{26}, \quad Signal = EMA_9(MACD)$$

Interpretation:

- MACD Line crossing above Signal Line = bullish signal.
- MACD Line crossing below Signal Line = bearish signal.
- Divergence with price can indicate trend reversal.

Example: MACD crosses above the signal line while the stock breaks above resistance. This could indicate a strong upward move.

Bollinger Bands

Bollinger Bands consist of a moving average (typically 20-period SMA) and upper/lower bands based on standard deviations (usually 2).

$$Upper\ Band = SMA + 2 \times \sigma, \quad Lower\ Band = SMA - 2 \times \sigma$$

Interpretation:

- Price near upper band = overbought; potential reversal or consolidation.
- Price near lower band = oversold; potential bounce.

- Band width indicates volatility: narrow bands = low volatility (possible breakout), wide bands = high volatility.

Example: A stock trades in a narrow band for weeks. A breakout above the upper band could indicate a strong trending move.

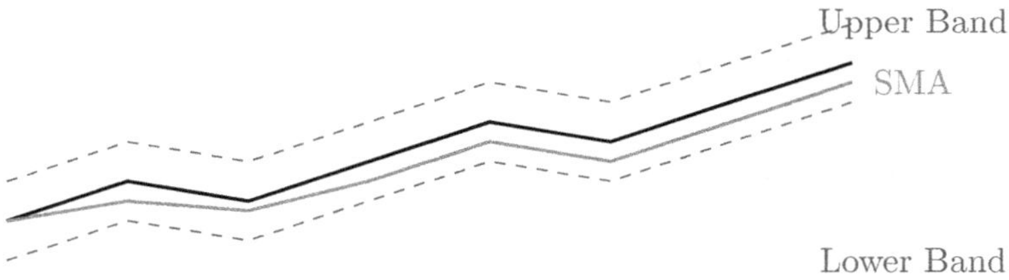

Key Takeaways

- RSI identifies overbought/oversold conditions and potential reversals.
- MACD tracks trend strength and momentum; crossovers provide entry/exit signals.
- Bollinger Bands measure volatility and highlight potential breakout zones.
- Combining indicators with price action improves trade probability.
- Avoid using too many indicators; focus on clarity and actionable signals.

5.3 Volume and Momentum Analysis

Understanding volume and momentum helps traders confirm trends, gauge strength, and anticipate reversals. Price alone can be misleading; combining it with volume and momentum indicators increases trade reliability.

Volume Analysis

Volume represents the number of shares, contracts, or units traded in a given period. **Key Points:**

- **Trend Confirmation:** Rising prices accompanied by high volume indicate a strong bullish trend. Falling prices with high volume indicate strong bearish pressure.

- **Breakouts:** Breakouts with low volume are often false. Look for volume spikes to validate moves.
- **Divergence:** Price making new highs while volume decreases may signal weakening momentum and potential reversal.

Example: A stock breaks above resistance at $100, but volume is 20% below the average daily volume. The breakout may not sustain.

Momentum Analysis

Momentum measures the speed of price changes to identify trend strength. Popular momentum indicators include:

- **Rate of Change (ROC):** Measures percentage change between current and past prices.
- **Stochastic Oscillator:** Compares closing price to price range over a set period; identifies overbought/oversold conditions.
- **Momentum Indicator:** Simply the difference between current and past prices.

Example: A stock is in an uptrend, but momentum is decreasing. This divergence suggests a potential slowing of the trend or a reversal.

Volume + Momentum Combination

Combining both provides a probabilistic edge:

- Price up + volume up + momentum rising = strong bullish trend.
- Price up + volume down + momentum falling = weak trend; caution advised.
- Price down + volume up + momentum falling = strong bearish trend.

Key Takeaways

- Volume confirms price trends and breakouts; watch for spikes or drops.
- Momentum gauges trend strength and potential reversals.
- Divergences between price, volume, and momentum often signal caution or opportunity.

- Use volume and momentum together to make probabilistic trade decisions.
- Avoid relying on a single metric; always combine with trend analysis and support/resistance levels.

5.4 Combining Indicators Without Overloading

Using multiple technical indicators can provide more confirmation for trades, but overloading charts with too many tools can create confusion and conflicting signals. The key is to select complementary indicators that enhance your probabilistic edge without overwhelming decision-making.

Principles of Indicator Combination

- **Complementary Indicators:** Combine indicators that measure different aspects of the market (e.g., trend + momentum + volume). Avoid using multiple indicators that give the same type of signal.
- **Simplicity Wins:** Focus on 2–4 key indicators for your strategy. More is not always better.
- **Avoid Redundancy:** Using RSI, Stochastic, and CCI together may produce overlapping overbought/oversold signals; pick one or two.
- **Context Matters:** Indicators work best when combined with price action, support/resistance levels, and market structure.

Suggested Indicator Combinations

- **Trend + Momentum:** Moving Average (trend) + RSI or MACD (momentum)
- **Trend + Volume:** EMA + volume spikes for breakout confirmation
- **Support/Resistance + Oscillator:** Trend lines + Stochastic for timing entries/exits

Example

Suppose a stock is above its 50-day EMA (uptrend) and RSI crosses from below 30 to above 30 (momentum turning bullish). This combination increases the probability of a profitable long trade.

Avoid adding too many oscillators or moving averages; conflicting signals can lead to hesitation, missed trades, or overtrading.

Practical Tips

- Keep a trading journal to track which combinations give consistent results.
- Regularly review indicator effectiveness; markets evolve.
- Focus on probabilistic confirmation, not certainty. Indicators increase the odds, not guarantee success.

Key Takeaways

- Combining indicators can improve trading decisions, but simplicity is crucial.
- Pick indicators that complement each other, covering trend, momentum, and volume.
- Avoid redundancy and conflicting signals.
- Indicators are tools to enhance probabilistic decision-making, not crystal balls.

Exercise: Backtest 5 Trades with Different Indicators

Objective: Evaluate how different technical indicators influence trade outcomes and develop a sense of probability and reliability.

1. Choose a market (stocks, forex, or crypto) and a timeframe (e.g., daily or 4-hour chart).
2. Select 5 different trades from historical data where you can apply different indicators such as:

- Moving Averages (SMA, EMA)
- RSI (Relative Strength Index)
- MACD (Moving Average Convergence Divergence)
- Bollinger Bands
- Volume or Momentum Indicators

3. Record the following for each trade:
   - Entry point and exit point
   - Indicator(s) used
   - Trade outcome (profit/loss)
   - Notes on market context and signals
4. Analyze patterns: Did certain indicators align better with successful trades? Did some conflict?
5. Summarize your findings and refine your approach for future trades.

Tip: Keep it simple—use only 2–3 indicators per trade. Focus on understanding patterns, not memorizing indicators.

Key Takeaways

- Technical indicators are tools derived from price, volume, or both, helping traders identify trends, momentum, and potential reversals.
- Moving averages (SMA, EMA) smooth out price data to reveal trend direction and potential support/resistance levels.
- RSI signals overbought or oversold conditions, indicating potential trend exhaustion or reversal points.
- MACD helps identify trend strength, direction, and momentum changes by analyzing the difference between moving averages.
- Bollinger Bands measure volatility and provide context for price extremes, highlighting potential breakout or reversal zones.
- Volume and momentum indicators confirm the strength of price moves and help distinguish between real trends and false signals.

- Combining indicators can improve decision-making, but overloading charts with too many signals can create confusion and conflicting information.
- Backtesting trades with different indicators helps traders understand which tools align best with their style and enhances probability-based decision-making.
- Consistent practice, record-keeping, and analysis are essential for mastering indicators and applying them effectively in real trading scenarios.

Chapter 6

Fundamental Analysis

Introduction

Fundamental analysis is the study of the intrinsic value of an asset by examining economic, financial, and qualitative factors. Unlike technical analysis, which focuses on price movements and patterns, fundamental analysis looks at the underlying business, its financial health, industry position, and broader economic indicators.

By understanding these factors, traders and investors can make informed decisions about whether an asset is undervalued, overvalued, or fairly priced, helping to manage long-term risk and identify opportunities.

A Story: Understanding the Business Behind the Price

Sameer, a beginner trader, often bought stocks based solely on charts. One day, he bought a company that looked strong technically, but its earnings report was disappointing. The stock fell sharply the next week. That's when he realized: behind every price is a business or asset with fundamentals that drive long-term value.

6.1 Reading Company Financials: Balance Sheet, P&L, Cash Flow

Understanding a company's financial statements is crucial for evaluating its health, profitability, and long-term potential. The three main statements are the **Balance Sheet**, the **Profit and Loss (P&L) Statement**, and the **Cash Flow Statement**.

1. Balance Sheet

The balance sheet shows a snapshot of a company's financial position at a specific point in time. It includes:

- **Assets:** What the company owns (cash, inventory, property, equipment).
- **Liabilities:** What the company owes (loans, accounts payable).
- **Equity:** The owners' share (Assets - Liabilities).

Example: AlphaTech Balance Sheet (in millions USD)

Assets	**Amount**
Cash	50
Inventory	30
Property	120
Total Assets	**200**
Liabilities	**Amount**
Loans	60
Accounts Payable	20
Total Liabilities	**80**
Equity	**120**

2. Profit & Loss (Income Statement)

The P&L shows revenues, expenses, and profit over a period (quarterly or yearly). Key components:

- **Revenue:** Money earned from sales.
- **Expenses:** Cost of goods sold, operating expenses, taxes.
- **Net Profit:** Revenue - Expenses.

Example: AlphaTech P&L (in millions USD)

Revenue	150
Cost of Goods Sold	90
Operating Expenses	30
Taxes	10
Net Profit	**20**

3. Cash Flow Statement

The cash flow statement tracks the actual inflow and outflow of cash. It is divided into:

- **Operating Activities:** Cash from core business operations.
- **Investing Activities:** Cash used for or from buying/selling assets.
- **Financing Activities:** Cash from loans, stock issuance, or dividends.

Example: AlphaTech Cash Flow (in millions USD)

Operating Cash Flow	25
Investing Cash Flow	-15
Financing Cash Flow	-5
Net Change in Cash	**5**

Key Takeaways

- The balance sheet shows what a company owns and owes at a point in time.
- The P&L indicates profitability and operational efficiency over a period.
- The cash flow statement reveals liquidity and the company's ability to fund operations or investments.
- Analyzing all three together gives a holistic picture of financial health.
- Always compare with past periods and industry peers to assess performance.

6.2 Ratios: P/E, ROE, Debt/Equity

Financial ratios are essential tools for analyzing a company's performance, efficiency, and financial health. They condense complex financial statements into understandable metrics and allow comparison across companies and industries. Understanding these ratios helps traders and investors make informed decisions, both for short-term trades and long-term investing.

1. Price-to-Earnings (P/E) Ratio

The P/E ratio shows how much investors are willing to pay for each dollar of earnings:

$$P/E = \frac{MarketPriceperShare}{EarningsperShare(EPS)}$$

Example: - Stock A trades at \$100 per share with EPS = \$5 → P/E = 20 - Stock B trades at \$50 per share with EPS = \$5 → P/E = 10

Interpretation: - Higher P/E (Stock A) suggests investors expect faster growth or are willing to pay a premium. - Lower P/E (Stock B) could indicate undervaluation or slower expected growth. - Important: Compare P/E within the same industry for context.

2. Return on Equity (ROE)

ROE measures a company's efficiency in generating profit from shareholders' equity:

$$ROE = \frac{NetIncome}{ShareholderEquity} \times 100\%$$

Example: - Company X: Net Income = \$2M, Equity = \$10M → ROE = 20% - Company Y: Net Income = \$1M, Equity = \$5M → ROE = 20%

Interpretation: - Both companies generate 20% return on equity. - A high ROE indicates efficient use of equity but check for excessive debt, which can inflate ROE artificially.

3. Debt-to-Equity (D/E) Ratio

The D/E ratio reflects the proportion of financing that comes from debt versus equity:

$$D/E = \frac{TotalLiabilities}{ShareholderEquity}$$

Example: - Company X: Liabilities = \$5M, Equity = \$10M → D/E = 0.5 - Company Y: Liabilities = \$15M, Equity = \$10M → D/E = 1.5

Interpretation: - Company Y relies more on debt, which increases financial risk but can also boost returns. - Company X is more conservatively financed, reducing risk but potentially limiting growth.

Putting It All Together

Analyzing these ratios together gives a clearer picture:

- Stock A: P/E = 20, ROE = 20%, D/E = 0.5 → healthy growth potential, moderate risk
- Stock B: P/E = 10, ROE = 20%, D/E = 1.5 → undervalued opportunity, but higher leverage risk

Practical Insight: - Use ratios as complementary tools, not in isolation. - Look for consistent performance across multiple ratios before committing capital. - Consider industry averages and macroeconomic factors to contextualize numbers.

Tip for Traders: - Short-term traders may focus on P/E for momentum plays. - Long-term investors should combine ROE and D/E with qualitative analysis of the business fundamentals.

Comparing Companies

Company	P/E Ratio	ROE (%)	Debt-to-Equity
AlphaTech	25	18	0.6
BetaCorp	15	22	1.2
GammaIndustries	20	15	0.4

Interpretation:

- **AlphaTech:** High P/E indicates growth expectations, moderate ROE, moderate debt → balanced risk/reward.
- **BetaCorp:** Lower P/E but higher ROE and high D/E → profitable but more leveraged, riskier.

- **GammaIndustries:** Moderate P/E, lower ROE, low debt → conservative, steady returns but slower growth.

Key Takeaway: Ratios provide a snapshot, but comparing multiple companies helps identify relative strengths, growth potential, and financial risk. Combine this with qualitative analysis and market context before making decisions.

6.3 Economic Indicators

Economic indicators are key statistics that reflect the health of an economy and influence financial markets. Traders and investors use these indicators to anticipate market moves, gauge economic strength, and adjust strategies accordingly.

Major Economic Indicators

- **Gross Domestic Product (GDP):** Measures the total economic output of a country over a specific period. A higher-than-expected GDP can signal a strong economy and drive stock and currency appreciation.
  Example: If the U.S. GDP grows 3% instead of the expected 2%, the USD and equities may rise on optimism.

- **Consumer Price Index (CPI) / Inflation:** Tracks changes in the price level of goods and services. High inflation can trigger central bank tightening, affecting bonds, stocks, and currencies.
  Example: A sudden CPI spike in India may strengthen the rupee if the RBI is expected to raise rates.

- **Non-Farm Payrolls (NFP):** Reports monthly U.S. employment excluding agriculture. It's a critical indicator of labor market strength.
  Example: A stronger-than-expected NFP report often boosts USD and equity markets, while weaker data may cause a sell-off.

- **Interest Rate Decisions:** Central banks set rates to control inflation and growth. Changes impact borrowing costs, market liquidity, and asset valuations.
  Example: An unexpected rate hike by the ECB can strengthen the euro and pressure European equities.

- **Retail Sales, Trade Balance, and PMI:** Provide insight into consumer spending, international trade, and manufacturing/ services health. *Example:* Rising retail sales in Australia may boost the AUD and consumer stocks.

How Traders Use Economic Indicators

1. **Forecast Market Moves:** By comparing actual releases to forecasts, traders anticipate short-term price movements.
2. **Risk Management:** Avoid holding positions before high-impact releases or use stop-losses to mitigate volatility.
3. **Strategy Development:** Integrate indicators into trend analysis, momentum strategies, or currency pair selection.

Example Scenario

Suppose EUR/USD is trading at 1.1000. The upcoming U.S. NFP report is forecasted at +200K jobs. The trader expects a strong report and places a trade:

- **Trade:** Buy EUR/USD anticipating USD strength.
- **Outcome:** NFP comes out at +250K — stronger than expected. The USD rises, EUR/USD falls to 1.0950. The trader's position incurs a loss, demonstrating the importance of understanding probability and market reaction.

Key Takeaways:

- Economic indicators are essential tools for forecasting potential market moves.
- Always consider forecasts vs. actual releases to assess probability and risk.
- Combine indicator analysis with technical and fundamental tools for better decision-making.

Example: Rising CPI may indicate inflation, leading central banks to hike interest rates, which can weaken equities and strengthen the currency.

6.4 News, Events, and Market Sentiment Analysis

Markets do not move only on numbers and charts — they also respond to **news, events, and investor sentiment.** The same company earnings or economic report can spark wildly different reactions depending on how traders *feel* about the future. Understanding how news and sentiment shape price action is crucial for short-term and long-term decision-making.

Impact of News and Events

- **Earnings Reports:** Strong or weak results can trigger rallies or sell-offs. *Example:* Apple announcing record iPhone sales often pushes its stock higher.
- **Economic Data Releases:** Reports like CPI (inflation), unemployment, or GDP growth can shift entire markets. *Example:* Higher-than-expected inflation usually causes bond yields to rise and stocks to fall.
- **Geopolitical Events:** Elections, wars, trade disputes, or natural disasters can spark uncertainty and volatility. *Example:* Oil prices often surge during Middle East conflicts due to supply concerns.
- **Policy Decisions:** Central bank actions (rate hikes or cuts, QE) heavily influence currencies, bonds, and equities.

Role of Market Sentiment

- **Positive Sentiment:** Optimism drives demand, often pushing prices beyond fair value.
- **Negative Sentiment:** Fear or panic can cause steep declines, even if fundamentals remain intact.
- **Herd Behavior:** Traders often follow the crowd, creating bubbles or crashes. **Example:** The 2021 GameStop rally fueled by social media hype, not fundamentals.

How Traders Analyze Sentiment

1. **Monitor News Flow:** Use financial news platforms (Bloomberg, Reuters, CNBC).

2. **Track Market Reactions:** Watch how prices respond to headlines — sometimes the market moves opposite to expectations.
3. **Use Sentiment Indicators:** Fear & Greed Index, VIX (volatility index), AAII investor surveys.
4. **Social Media Analysis:** Platforms like Twitter (X), Reddit, and StockTwits amplify retail investor psychology.

Example Scenario

Imagine unemployment data comes out stronger than expected (fewer jobless claims):

- Stocks may rise because strong jobs suggest a healthy economy.
- Bonds may fall as traders anticipate interest rate hikes.
- Sentiment shifts quickly — if markets were already overly optimistic, the reaction could be muted or even negative.

Key Takeaways

- News and events act as catalysts for market moves.
- Sentiment amplifies reactions, often overshooting fundamentals.
- Traders must distinguish between temporary noise and lasting impact.
- Best practice: combine news/event analysis with technical and fundamental tools before making decisions.

Case Study: Apple Stock Pre-iPhone Launch

Sometimes, history provides the clearest lessons in how fundamentals, innovation, and sentiment converge to shape markets. Apple Inc. offers a prime example.

Background

In the early 2000s, Apple was best known for its iPod and Mac computers. By 2006, the company was profitable but far from the trillion-dollar giant it is today. Analysts and investors debated whether Apple could expand beyond its niche markets.

The Event

On January 9, 2007, Steve Jobs unveiled the first iPhone at the Macworld Conference. The announcement was revolutionary — a phone, music player, and internet device combined into one sleek product. This was not just a new gadget; it was the birth of a new ecosystem.

Market Reaction

- **Before the Launch:** Apple's stock (AAPL) traded around $10 (split-adjusted). Sentiment was cautiously optimistic but uncertain about long-term adoption.
- **After the Launch:** Within 12 months, Apple's share price doubled as sales exceeded expectations. Investors realized the company had transformed from a computer brand into a consumer electronics powerhouse.
- **Long-Term Impact:** By 2012, the iPhone accounted for more than half of Apple's revenue, and the stock price had climbed above $80 (split-adjusted). Apple's fundamentals — revenue growth, profit margins, and global market share — all strengthened dramatically.

Lessons Learned

1. **Innovation Drives Fundamentals:** A single breakthrough product can redefine a company's financial trajectory.
2. **Market Sentiment Matters:** Investor skepticism often lingers until proof of adoption emerges — creating opportunities for early believers.
3. **Events as Catalysts:** Major product launches, much like earnings or policy announcements, can act as turning points in a stock's history.

This case study shows how combining **fundamental analysis** (revenue potential), **sentiment analysis** (investor expectations), and **event-driven awareness** (iPhone launch) can provide a powerful edge.

Exercise: Analyze a Company or Currency Using Fundamentals

To strengthen your understanding of fundamental analysis, try this hands-on exercise:

Step 1: Select an Asset

Choose one of the following:

- A publicly listed company (e.g., Tesla, Infosys, or Apple).
- A currency pair (e.g., USD/INR, EUR/USD).

Step 2: Gather Data

- For a **company**: Find the latest balance sheet, profit & loss statement, and cash flow report. Look for revenue growth, profitability, and debt levels.
- For a **currency**: Look up key macroeconomic indicators such as GDP growth, interest rates, inflation, and central bank policy.

Step 3: Apply Ratios or Indicators

- Company: Calculate at least 2 ratios such as P/E, ROE, or Debt/Equity.
- Currency: Identify whether current interest rate differentials or inflation trends support strength or weakness.

Step 4: Interpret the Results

- What do the numbers tell you about the asset's health?
- Are there red flags (e.g., high debt, slowing growth, weak GDP)?
- What does sentiment or recent news say about it?

Step 5: Write a Short Summary

Conclude with 3–5 sentences: "Based on fundamentals, I believe ___ is undervalued/overvalued because ___. Key drivers include ___, and risks are ___."

This simple framework mirrors what analysts and traders do every day to build conviction before making a decision.

Sample 1: Tesla (Company Analysis)

Step 1: Select an Asset Tesla Inc. (Ticker: TSLA).

Step 2: Gather Data (Simplified Example)

- Revenue (2023): \$96 billion (up 19% YoY).
- Net Income (2023): \$15 billion.
- Total Debt: \$5 billion.
- Shareholder Equity: \$60 billion.
- Market Cap: \$700 billion.

Step 3: Apply Ratios

- Price-to-Earnings (P/E) = 700B / 15B 46.7 → High, suggests premium valuation.
- Return on Equity (ROE) = 15B / 60B = 25% → Strong profitability.
- Debt/Equity = 5B / 60B = 0.08 → Very low leverage.

Step 4: Interpretation Tesla is highly profitable with low debt and strong ROE, but the P/E ratio indicates the stock is priced for significant future growth. Any slowdown in revenue could trigger a sharp correction.

Step 5: Summary "Tesla appears financially healthy with strong ROE and low debt. However, its high P/E ratio suggests overvaluation unless growth continues at a fast pace. Risk: slower EV adoption or increased competition."

Sample 2: USD/INR (Currency Analysis)

Step 1: Select an Asset Currency Pair: US Dollar vs. Indian Rupee.

Step 2: Gather Data (Simplified Example)

- US GDP Growth: 2.4% (2023).
- India GDP Growth: 6.5% (2023).
- US Inflation: 3.2%.
- India Inflation: 5.5%.
- US Fed Interest Rate: 5.25%.
- RBI Repo Rate: 6.5%.

Step 3: Apply Indicators

- Higher GDP growth in India supports a stronger INR.

- Higher inflation in India offsets some of that strength.
- Interest rate differential (RBI 6.5% vs. Fed 5.25%) attracts capital inflows into India.

Step 4: Interpretation USD/INR may face downward pressure (stronger INR) if India continues strong growth and attracts foreign investment. However, risks include oil import costs, global risk aversion, or US Fed tightening.

Step 5: Summary "Fundamentals suggest the INR has room to strengthen given higher growth and rates, but structural risks (inflation, oil prices, global volatility) could limit upside."

Key Takeaways

- Fundamental analysis looks beyond charts and prices — it studies the **business, economy, and sentiment** that drive long-term value.
- Company financials (Balance Sheet, P&L, Cash Flow) reveal **profitability, debt levels, and cash health**.
- Ratios like **P/E, ROE, and Debt/Equity** provide quick comparisons between companies.
- **Economic indicators** (GDP, inflation, interest rates, employment) shape overall market direction.
- **Sentiment and news** can cause short-term volatility, even when fundamentals are strong.
- Combining fundamentals with technicals creates a more **balanced view** for decision-making.
- Always assess the **risk vs. reward** and remember: even strong fundamentals do not guarantee short-term price moves.

Chapter 7

Trading Platforms & Tools

Introduction

Every trader needs more than just capital and knowledge — they need the right **platform and tools**. A trading platform is the bridge between you and the market, where decisions turn into real trades. The difference between a simple broker app and a professional-grade platform can determine how efficiently you execute strategies, manage risk, and track performance.

In this chapter, we'll explore how to choose the right broker, evaluate trading platforms, and make use of essential tools such as alerts, watchlists, and dashboards. By the end, you'll understand how technology can give you a practical edge in your trading journey.

A Story: The Right Tools Make a Difference

Riya started trading on a basic broker app. She quickly realized she missed opportunities because she couldn't set alerts, track multiple instruments, or analyze charts efficiently. A proper trading platform with advanced tools can improve execution, reduce mistakes, and help a trader act on signals faster.

7.1 Choosing a Broker: Fees, Regulation, Execution

Your broker is your gateway to the financial markets. Choosing the wrong one can cost you money, time, and even trust in the system. The right broker should provide fair fees, proper regulation, and reliable trade execution. Let's break these down:

1. Fees and Commissions

Brokers make money through spreads, commissions, or hidden costs.

- **Spreads:** The difference between the bid and ask price. Tight spreads are better for active traders.
- **Commissions:** Some brokers charge a flat fee or a per-trade fee. Others are "commission-free" but widen spreads.
- **Other Costs:** Overnight financing (swap rates), account inactivity fees, and withdrawal charges.

Example: If a broker charges a $5 commission per trade, and you trade 20 times per month, that's $100 in fees — regardless of profit or loss. For active traders, fee structure can significantly affect net returns.

2. Regulation and Safety

Always ensure your broker is regulated by a recognized authority. Regulation protects traders from fraud and ensures transparency.

- U.S.: Securities and Exchange Commission (SEC), FINRA, CFTC.
- U.K.: Financial Conduct Authority (FCA).
- Europe: European Securities and Markets Authority (ESMA).
- India: Securities and Exchange Board of India (SEBI).

Tip: Avoid unregulated offshore brokers, even if they promise high leverage or bonuses. Safety of funds is more important than perks.

3. Execution Speed and Reliability

Fast, accurate order execution is critical for traders, especially in volatile markets.

- **Execution Models:** Market maker vs. ECN/STP (direct market access). ECN/STP often provide better transparency and faster fills.

- **Slippage:** The difference between expected and actual execution price. Good brokers minimize slippage.
- **Platform Stability:** Downtime during major news events can cost traders dearly. Choose a broker with a reputation for uptime and reliability.

Checklist for Choosing a Broker

1. Are fees and commissions clear and competitive?
2. Is the broker regulated by a trusted authority?
3. Does it offer fast execution with minimal slippage?
4. Are trading platforms and mobile apps stable and user-friendly?
5. Are there hidden costs (withdrawals, inactivity, overnight fees)?

Key Point: A good broker should make trading easier, not harder. Focus on transparency, safety, and execution — profits depend on it.

7.2 Trading Software: MT4/MT5, TradingView, Thinkorswim

A trading platform is more than just a screen to place trades — it is the trader's workstation. The choice of software can directly impact efficiency, analysis, and decision-making. Here are some of the most widely used platforms:

1. MetaTrader 4 (MT4) and MetaTrader 5 (MT5)

- **Overview:** MT4 and MT5 are among the most popular trading platforms, especially for Forex and CFDs. They are lightweight, fast, and widely supported by brokers.
- **Key Features:**
  - Advanced charting with multiple timeframes.
  - Support for automated trading (Expert Advisors).
  - Large community and thousands of custom indicators.

- **Difference:** MT4 is simpler and Forex-focused, while MT5 supports more markets (stocks, commodities) and offers improved backtesting tools.

Example: A Forex trader can set up an Expert Advisor on MT4 to automatically execute trades when RSI crosses a certain level, eliminating emotional bias.

2. TradingView

- **Overview:** A web-based platform known for its clean interface, interactive charts, and social community features.
- **Key Features:**
  - Powerful charting tools with hundreds of indicators.
  - Pine Script for building custom strategies.
  - Social trading community where users share charts and trade ideas.
  - Accessible from browser and mobile without heavy installation.
- **Best For:** Technical analysis enthusiasts and traders who want flexibility across multiple devices.

Example: A trader identifies a *head and shoulders* pattern on TradingView, shares it with the community, and receives feedback from other traders before making a decision.

3. Thinkorswim (TOS) by TD Ameritrade

- **Overview:** A professional-grade platform tailored for active stock and options traders.
- **Key Features:**
  - Advanced option chains and derivatives analysis.
  - Paper trading (simulate trades without real money).
  - Built-in scanners for stocks, ETFs, and options.
  - Strong educational resources and integration with TD Ameritrade accounts.

- **Best For:** U.S. equity and options traders who need in-depth analysis and execution tools.

Example: An options trader uses Thinkorswim's probability analysis tool to evaluate the chance of an option expiring in-the-money before executing a spread trade.

Choosing the Right Platform

- If you want automated trading and broker flexibility: **MT4/MT5**.
- If you prioritize clean charts, social sharing, and accessibility: **TradingView**.
- If you trade U.S. stocks and options with advanced analytics: **Thinkorswim**.

Tip: Many traders combine platforms — for example, analyzing on TradingView and executing trades on MT4/MT5.

7.3 Setting Alerts, Watchlists, and Dashboards

Successful trading is not about watching charts all day—it's about making informed decisions at the right time. Alerts, watchlists, and dashboards are tools that help traders monitor multiple instruments, spot opportunities, and react efficiently.

1. Alerts

- **Purpose:** Automatically notify you when price levels, technical indicators, or news events meet predefined conditions.
- **Types of Alerts:**
  - **Price Alerts:** Trigger when an asset crosses a specific price threshold.
  - **Indicator Alerts:** Trigger when RSI, MACD, Bollinger Bands, or other indicators reach certain values.
  - **News/Events Alerts:** Notify when economic releases, earnings reports, or significant company announcements occur.

- **Example:** A trader sets an alert for Bitcoin crossing $35,000. When triggered, they can review charts, assess momentum, and decide whether to enter or exit the market.

2. Watchlists

- **Purpose:** Track multiple instruments simultaneously in a single, organized list.
- **Benefits:** Quickly compare performance, spot correlations, and manage portfolio risk.
- **Example:** A trader monitors a watchlist of tech stocks (Apple, Tesla, Microsoft) alongside cryptocurrencies (BTC, ETH, ADA), observing trends, volatility, and relative performance to prioritize trades.

3. Dashboards

- **Purpose:** Provide a consolidated, at-a-glance overview of market data, open positions, alerts, and portfolio metrics.
- **Components:**
  - Live price charts with indicators and trend signals.
  - Open trades, order status, and margin usage.
  - Performance metrics such as P&L, exposure, and risk levels.
- **Example:** A trader monitors five open trades across stocks, forex, and crypto. The dashboard shows real-time P&L, stop-loss alerts, and trend indicators, enabling faster, data-driven decisions.

Key Takeaway

Properly configured alerts, watchlists, and dashboards transform trading from reactive to proactive. They allow traders to act on opportunities, maintain discipline, and manage multiple instruments effectively—without being glued to the screen all day.

Exercise: Platform Setup

Objective: Familiarize yourself with trading platforms and tools.

1. Choose a broker and open a demo account.
2. Install a trading platform (MT4/MT5, TradingView, Thinkorswim).
3. Set up watchlists for 5–10 instruments.
4. Create price alerts and notifications.
5. Practice placing market, limit, and stop orders on the demo account.

Exercise: Set Up Your Trading Platform with Alerts

This exercise will help you practice using your trading platform efficiently by setting up alerts, watchlists, and dashboards.

1. **Choose a Trading Platform:** Pick a platform such as TradingView, MT4/MT5, or Thinkorswim.
2. **Create a Watchlist:** Add at least 5 instruments (stocks, forex pairs, or crypto) that you want to track.
3. **Set Alerts:**
    - Price alert for when an asset crosses a target price.
    - Indicator alert for RSI, MACD, or moving averages.
    - Optional: News/event alert for significant economic announcements.
4. **Configure Dashboard:** Arrange charts, indicators, and open positions for a clear overview.
5. **Record Observations:** Use a trading journal to note:
    - Which alerts triggered and how you responded.
    - How the watchlist and dashboard helped monitor the market.
    - Any difficulties or insights gained while using the tools.
6. **Review & Adjust:** After a few days, refine alerts, watchlists, and dashboards for optimal efficiency.

Goal: By the end of this exercise, you should be comfortable using alerts, watchlists, and dashboards to manage trades effectively without constantly staring at the screen.

Key Takeaways

- Efficient trading requires tools to monitor markets without being glued to screens.
- **Alerts** notify you of price levels, indicator signals, or news events, allowing timely decisions.
- **Watchlists** help you track multiple instruments, compare performance, and spot correlations quickly.
- **Dashboards** consolidate market data, open positions, and portfolio metrics for a comprehensive overview.
- Combining these tools enables proactive trading, reduces missed opportunities, and improves discipline.
- Regularly reviewing and configuring your alerts, watchlists, and dashboards ensures they remain aligned with your trading strategy.

Part III

Core Trading Concepts

Chapter 8

Probability in Trading

Introduction

Trading is not about certainty — it is about making decisions under uncertainty. Many traders fail because they look for guarantees in a system that is inherently unpredictable. Markets are influenced by countless factors — economic data, investor sentiment, global events — most of which cannot be controlled.

This chapter focuses on applying **probability as a decision-making framework**. By shifting from "Will this trade win?" to "What is the likelihood of different outcomes, and is the potential reward worth the risk?", traders begin to think like professionals.

In the following sections, we will explore how probability connects to risk, reward, and statistical thinking — and how it can be used to build a true trading edge.

8.1 Understanding Probability in Markets

Probability is the backbone of trading and investing. Every trade you place is essentially a bet on an uncertain future. Probability gives you the language and tools to evaluate uncertainty and make rational, consistent decisions. Without it, traders fall into the trap of prediction, hope, and emotional reactions — all of which can destroy long-term results.

Why Probability Matters

Financial markets are complex, adaptive systems influenced by countless variables:

- Macroeconomic data (inflation, interest rates, GDP growth).
- Company fundamentals (earnings, balance sheets, management decisions).
- Market psychology (fear, greed, herd behavior).
- Random shocks (geopolitical events, natural disasters, black swan events).

No trader can predict all these factors. But probability helps you answer the most important question: *"Given what I know, what is the likelihood of different outcomes, and does the potential reward justify the risk?"*

Prediction vs. Probability

Many traders confuse these concepts:

- **Prediction:** "The market will rise tomorrow." (A binary, overconfident statement).
- **Probability:** "Based on past setups, there is a 60% chance this trade works, with a 2:1 reward-to-risk ratio." (A measured, data-driven statement).

The probabilistic trader accepts uncertainty. They do not seek to be "right" every time; they seek to have a consistent edge over time.

Sources of Probabilities in Trading

Traders estimate probabilities through multiple approaches:

1. **Historical Performance:** Backtesting a strategy across years of data to measure win rates.
2. **Statistical Tools:** Using variance, standard deviation, and probability distributions to quantify risk.
3. **Options Market Data:** Implied volatility reflects the market's collective expectation of future movement.

4. **Patterns and Setups:** Chart patterns and technical indicators provide probabilistic edges when validated by data.

5. **Bayesian Updating:** Adjusting probabilities as new information (earnings, news, macro events) arrives.

Illustrative Example: Coin Toss vs. Trading

- A coin toss has a 50% chance of heads and 50% chance of tails. This probability is fixed and known.
- A trade setup, say a breakout, may have a 55–60% chance of success based on historical testing. But unlike a coin toss, this probability is dynamic, changing as conditions shift.

The trader's role is to recognize when probabilities tilt in their favor.

Expected Value and Probability in Action

Imagine a breakout strategy with the following stats:

- Win rate: 55%
- Average win: $200
- Average loss: $100

The expected value (EV) is:

$$EV = (0.55 \times 200) + (0.45 \times -100) = 110 - 45 = 65$$

This means that, on average, every trade has a statistical value of $65. Even though the strategy loses 45% of the time, it is profitable over the long run.

Common Probability Traps

1. **The Gambler's Fallacy:** Believing that past outcomes influence future independent events. ("The stock has fallen five days in a row, so it must rise tomorrow.")

2. **The Illusion of Certainty:** Mistaking high probability for certainty. (A 90% chance still means 1 in 10 times you will be wrong).

3. **Overfitting:** Designing strategies that work only on past data but fail in real markets.

4. **Ignoring Changing Conditions:** Probabilities are dynamic, not fixed. A setup that worked in low volatility may fail in high volatility.

Practical Application for Traders

Before entering a trade, ask yourself:

1. What are the possible outcomes (up, down, sideways)?

2. What probability do I assign to each outcome?

3. What is my potential reward if I am right, and what is my risk if I am wrong?

4. Does the expected value of this trade justify the risk?

Exercise: Assign Probabilities to a Trade

Choose a stock, forex pair, or crypto asset you follow. Based on your analysis:

- Assign a probability to a bullish outcome, bearish outcome, and sideways outcome.
- Define your stop loss and take profit levels.
- Calculate the expected value (EV) of the trade.

This practice shifts your mindset from prediction to probabilistic reasoning.

Key Takeaways

- Markets are uncertain; probability is the rational framework for navigating that uncertainty.
- Probability is not prediction. It accepts multiple possible outcomes and prepares you for them.
- Probabilities in trading are estimated through data, patterns, models, and market information.
- Expected value (EV) is more important than win rate — a low win rate strategy can still be profitable if the average reward outweighs the risk.

- Common errors include gambler's fallacy, overconfidence, and overfitting historical data.
- Thinking in probabilities helps traders stay disciplined, avoid emotional decisions, and achieve consistency over the long run.

8.2 Risk, Reward, and Expected Value

At the heart of every trading decision lies a fundamental question: *Is this trade worth taking?* To answer it, traders must weigh the potential risk against the potential reward. Successful trading is not about winning every trade, but about ensuring that—over the long run—the rewards outweigh the risks. This requires a deep understanding of probability, expected value, and the discipline to act only when the numbers are in your favor.

Risk Defined:

Risk refers to the amount a trader is willing to lose if a trade goes against them. It is typically determined in advance, often by setting a stop-loss order. For example, if you buy a stock at $100 and place a stop-loss at $95, your risk per share is $5.

Reward Defined:

Reward is the potential profit a trader aims to capture if the trade moves in their favor. Continuing the example, if you set a profit target at $110, your reward per share is $10.

The Risk-to-Reward Ratio (R:R):

The relationship between risk and reward is expressed as a ratio. In the above example:

$$R : R = \frac{PotentialReward}{PotentialRisk} = \frac{10}{5} = 2 : 1$$

This means you stand to gain twice as much as you are willing to lose.

Expected Value (EV):

Expected value is a probabilistic measure that evaluates the average outcome of a trade if it were repeated many times. The formula is:

$$EV = (P_{win} \times R_{win}) - (P_{loss} \times R_{loss})$$

Where: - P_{win} = probability of winning - R_{win} = reward from a winning trade - P_{loss} = probability of losing (1 - P_{win}) - R_{loss} = risk from a losing trade

Example:
Suppose you take a trade with: - Risk = \$100 - Reward = \$200 - Probability of winning = 40%

The EV is:

$$EV = (0.4 \times 200) - (0.6 \times 100) = 80 - 60 = +20$$

Even though you win less than half the time, the trade has a **positive expected value**, meaning that over many trades, you would expect to make money.

Why Expected Value Matters:
Most traders focus only on whether they are "right" or "wrong." But profitability comes from consistency with positive-EV setups, not from being right every time. A trader who wins 70% of trades with a poor risk-to-reward ratio (e.g., risking \$100 to make \$50) can still lose money, while a trader who wins only 40% of trades but maintains a strong ratio (e.g., risking \$100 to make \$300) can be profitable in the long run.

Managing Risk and Reward Dynamically:
- Adjust position sizes to keep risk consistent across trades. - Let winners run when probabilities increase in your favor. - Cut losers quickly when evidence suggests the thesis is invalid. - Avoid trades where the expected value is negative, even if they "feel right."

Key Takeaways:

- Risk is the maximum amount you are willing to lose; reward is the potential profit you aim to achieve.
- The risk-to-reward ratio helps evaluate whether a trade is worth taking.
- Expected value (EV) combines probability with R:R to determine whether a strategy is profitable over the long run.
- A low win rate can still lead to profitability if the reward outweighs the risk.
- Consistently seeking positive-EV trades is the foundation of successful, probabilistic trading.

8.3 Statistical Thinking for Traders

Trading is not about predicting with certainty; it is about making decisions under uncertainty. To thrive in this environment, traders must adopt a **statistical mindset**. This means shifting from "Will this trade win or lose?" to "What is the probability distribution of outcomes, and how can I position myself to benefit from it?"

Statistical thinking transforms trading from an emotional activity into a disciplined process grounded in data, probabilities, and repeatable logic.

The Law of Large Numbers:
A single trade is subject to randomness. But across a large sample of trades, the results converge to the expected value of the strategy. Just as a coin flipped 10 times may land heads 7 times, flipping it 1,000 times will likely result in a distribution closer to 50/50. Traders must think in terms of **series of trades**, not individual outcomes.

Variance and Distribution of Returns:
Trading outcomes are not linear; they follow distributions. Some strategies produce frequent small wins with occasional large losses (high variance), while others deliver fewer but larger wins. Understanding whether your system has a fat-tailed distribution, high skew, or clustering of losses helps in preparing psychologically and financially.

Sample Size and Reliability:
One of the biggest mistakes traders make is drawing strong conclusions from too few trades. A strategy that appears profitable after 20 trades may fail after 200. Statistical thinking requires recognizing that the reliability of results increases with larger sample sizes, reducing the influence of short-term luck.

Avoiding Cognitive Biases:
Human intuition is poorly equipped to handle randomness. Traders often fall prey to:

- *Recency bias:* Overweighting recent results, assuming short-term outcomes reflect long-term probabilities.
- *Confirmation bias:* Interpreting data selectively to confirm a pre-existing belief about a strategy.
- *Gambler's fallacy:* Believing a loss streak makes a win "due."

Statistical thinking protects against these biases by forcing traders to anchor decisions in data rather than emotion.

Probabilities, Not Certainties:
No setup guarantees profit. Instead of searching for a "perfect signal," traders should evaluate:

- Probability of success (P_{win})
- Probability of failure (P_{loss})
- Expected reward vs. expected risk

By combining these factors, the trader focuses on managing risk and maximizing edge rather than seeking certainty.
Practical Applications of Statistical Thinking:

- Backtesting strategies on large datasets to reveal statistical properties.
- Using Monte Carlo simulations to model different market conditions and assess robustness.
- Tracking metrics like win rate, average win/loss, risk-adjusted return, and drawdown consistency.
- Thinking in probabilities when setting stop-losses, targets, and position sizing.

Case Study: Applying Probability to Find an Edge

Trader: Alex, a part-time forex trader

Scenario: Alex trades EUR/USD and notices a pattern where the currency often rises after specific economic releases. He evaluates the probability:

- 65% chance EUR/USD rises \$50 within 2 hours
- 35% chance it falls \$30 within 2 hours

Expected Value Calculation:

$$EV = (0.65 \times 50) + (0.35 \times -30) = 32.5 - 10.5 = 22$$

Decision: Since EV is positive (\$22 on average per trade), Alex executes the trade, maintaining strict stop-loss and risk limits.

Outcome: Even if individual trades lose, consistently applying this probability-based approach gives Alex a statistical edge over time.

Key Takeaways:

- Statistical thinking shifts focus from individual trades to long-term probabilities and distributions.
- The law of large numbers ensures that edge emerges over many trades, not in isolated outcomes.
- Sample size matters — the more trades analyzed, the more reliable the conclusion.
- Recognizing variance, fat tails, and skew prepares traders for the real-world behavior of markets.
- Data-driven decisions protect against cognitive biases and lead to consistency.

8.4 Using Probability to Build an Edge

In trading, success is not about predicting the future with certainty but about consistently identifying and exploiting situations where the **odds are in your favor**. This is what traders mean when they talk about having an "edge." An edge is not a guarantee of profit on every trade, but a repeatable advantage that produces positive results over time. Probability is the foundation for finding, testing, and sustaining that edge.

What is an Edge?

An edge is any factor that increases the likelihood of making profitable trades compared to random chance. It could be:

- A technical pattern that historically has a higher-than-average probability of success.
- A statistical tendency, such as mean reversion or momentum, supported by data.
- A psychological advantage, like the discipline to follow rules while others panic.

Without an edge, trading is gambling; with an edge, trading becomes a probabilistic game where discipline compounds the advantage.

Identifying Probabilistic Edges: To use probability as a tool for building an edge, traders must analyze strategies and quantify their statistical properties:

- *Win rate:* What percentage of trades historically end in profit?
- *Reward-to-risk ratio (R:R):* How much is gained on average relative to what is risked?
- *Expected value (EV):* Combining win rate and R:R into a single measure of long-term profitability.
- *Distribution analysis:* Looking beyond averages to understand variance, streaks, and fat tails.

Example:
Suppose a strategy has a 40% win rate, with an average win of \$300 and an average loss of \$100.

$$EV = (0.40 \times 300) - (0.60 \times 100) = 120 - 60 = +\$60 per trade$$

Even with fewer winners than losers, the strategy has a positive edge. Over 100 trades, the law of large numbers suggests profits will converge around +\$6,000, despite short-term variance.
Refining the Edge: Probability-driven traders don't stop at identifying an edge — they refine and stress-test it. This includes:

- Backtesting across different market regimes (bull, bear, sideways).
- Running Monte Carlo simulations to account for random sequencing of wins and losses.
- Tracking real-world performance in a trading journal to confirm the statistical edge holds.
- Adjusting position sizing and risk exposure to maximize returns while surviving inevitable drawdowns.

Edge + Discipline = Long-Term Success
An edge without discipline is useless. Traders must stick to their strategy long enough for probabilities to play out. Quitting after a losing streak or overleveraging after a win streak destroys the advantage. The key is consistency: executing the same process repeatedly, confident that the edge will emerge over time.

Key Takeaways:

- An edge is a repeatable, probabilistic advantage that separates trading from gambling.
- Probability provides the framework for identifying, quantifying, and refining that edge.
- Expected value (EV) is the ultimate measure of whether a system is profitable over time.
- Even a low win rate can be profitable if reward-to-risk is favorable.
- Discipline ensures the edge plays out — without it, probability never has time to work.

Key Takeaways

- Trading is inherently uncertain; probability provides a framework to make informed decisions rather than relying on luck.
- Every trade has a probability distribution of potential outcomes — understanding this helps quantify risk and expected reward.
- Risk, reward, and expected value (EV) are central concepts: EV determines whether a strategy is profitable over time, not individual trade outcomes.
- Statistical thinking allows traders to analyze patterns, backtest strategies, and evaluate the likelihood of different scenarios.
- Probabilistic analysis helps separate skill from randomness, enabling data-driven decision-making.
- An edge is any repeatable advantage that gives positive expected value; even low win-rate strategies can be profitable if reward-to-risk is favorable.
- Discipline and consistency are required for probabilities to play out — executing a system over many trades reduces the impact of short-term variance.
- Monitoring, journaling, and refining strategies are essential for maintaining an edge in changing market conditions.

- Thinking in odds helps manage emotions: losses are expected, and gains are probabilistic, reducing fear and overconfidence.

Chapter 9

Behavioral Finance

Introduction

Even the most well-designed trading strategies can fail if human psychology is ignored. Markets are driven not only by data and fundamentals, but also by the emotions, biases, and collective behavior of participants. Understanding these psychological factors is crucial to avoid costly mistakes and make better decisions under uncertainty.

This chapter explores **behavioral finance**, focusing on how cognitive biases, emotional traps, and herd behavior influence market outcomes. By recognizing these tendencies in yourself and others, you can develop strategies to mitigate their impact, stay disciplined, and make more rational trading decisions.

9.1 Cognitive Biases and Market Psychology

Markets are not purely rational. Even professional traders are susceptible to cognitive biases — systematic errors in thinking that influence decisions. Recognizing these biases is critical because they can lead to overtrading, poor risk management, and emotional decision-making.

Common Cognitive Biases in Trading

- **Confirmation Bias:** The tendency to seek information that confirms your existing beliefs while ignoring contradictory evidence. *Example:*

Believing a stock will rise, a trader only reads positive news and disregards warning signs.

- **Overconfidence Bias:** Overestimating your knowledge or predictive ability. *Example:* A trader takes larger positions than appropriate because they believe their system is infallible.
- **Anchoring Bias:** Relying too heavily on the first piece of information received. *Example:* A trader anchors on a stock's previous high and expects it to repeat, ignoring current market conditions.
- **Recency Bias:** Giving undue weight to recent events. *Example:* After a winning streak, a trader assumes their luck or skill will continue indefinitely.
- **Loss Aversion:** Feeling the pain of losses more strongly than the pleasure of gains. *Example:* Holding onto losing positions to avoid realizing a loss, which may worsen outcomes.
- **Hindsight Bias:** Believing past events were predictable after they have occurred. *Example:* Claiming "I knew it would happen" after a market crash, which can create false confidence in future predictions.

Psychology of the Crowd

- Markets reflect the collective psychology of all participants. Herd behavior occurs when traders follow the majority rather than independent analysis. *Example:* Buying a popular crypto during a hype cycle without understanding fundamentals.
- Sentiment can create bubbles or panics, often amplifying price moves beyond intrinsic value.

Managing Biases

- Keep a trading journal to record decisions and emotional state.
- Use checklists to enforce objective criteria before entering trades.
- Apply probabilistic thinking: focus on risk/reward and expected value, not certainty.
- Periodically review trades to identify patterns of bias in your behavior.

Example: Recognizing Confirmation Bias

A trader believes TechCorp will soar due to AI adoption. They read only positive news and ignore warnings of regulatory scrutiny. By keeping a journal and reviewing opposing viewpoints, they realize they were biased and adjust their position size, avoiding a potential large loss.

Key Takeaways

- Cognitive biases subtly influence decision-making and can lead to costly mistakes.
- Awareness and structured processes (journals, checklists, probabilistic thinking) mitigate bias.
- Crowd psychology and sentiment can create opportunities and risks; understanding them improves market timing and risk management.
- Regular self-reflection is essential to develop discipline and consistent trading behavior.

9.2 Emotional Traps and Herd Behavior

Trading is as much a test of emotions as it is of strategy. Even well-planned trades can fail if emotions dominate decision-making. Emotional traps are patterns of thinking and behavior that cause traders to make irrational decisions, while herd behavior occurs when individuals follow the majority instead of independent analysis.

Common Emotional Traps

- **Fear of Missing Out (FOMO):** The anxiety of missing a profitable opportunity can lead to impulsive entries at poor prices. *Example:* Buying a cryptocurrency at its all-time high because everyone else is buying, ignoring overvaluation risks.
- **Revenge Trading:** Trying to recover losses by taking larger or riskier positions. *Example:* After a losing trade, a trader doubles their position to break even, often resulting in even larger losses.

- **Overtrading:** Trading excessively due to boredom, excitement, or the urge to "make up" for losses. *Example:* Entering multiple trades without a solid plan or confirmation from indicators.
- **Anchoring to Emotions:** Letting recent emotions dictate trades instead of market data. *Example:* Holding a losing stock because selling feels emotionally painful.

Herd Behavior in Markets

- Traders often follow the crowd instead of independent analysis. Herd behavior can amplify price trends, creating bubbles or crashes. *Example:* Buying a stock simply because institutional investors are accumulating it, without understanding the fundamentals.
- Social media, news, and market hype accelerate herd behavior, making it difficult for traders to act rationally.
- Recognizing when the market is driven by emotion rather than fundamentals allows contrarian strategies to succeed.

Strategies to Avoid Emotional Traps

- **Predefined Trading Plan:** Define entry, exit, and risk parameters before trading to prevent impulsive decisions.
- **Position Sizing:** Limit exposure to any single trade to reduce emotional pressure.
- **Journaling:** Track emotions during trades and analyze patterns over time.
- **Pause Before Action:** Take a step back when feeling emotionally charged; avoid impulsive decisions.
- **Independent Analysis:** Base trades on research, indicators, and probability rather than the crowd.

Example: Avoiding FOMO in a Bubble

During a rapid tech stock rally, a trader feels pressure as colleagues and social media hype the gains. Instead of buying immediately, they review historical valuations, analyze earnings, and consult their trading plan. They choose to wait for a pullback, avoiding entry at an inflated price and mitigating risk.

Key Takeaways

- Emotions like fear, greed, and frustration can lead to costly mistakes if not managed.
- Herd behavior often drives extreme market moves; being aware of it can present both risks and opportunities.
- Structured plans, journaling, and independent analysis help mitigate emotional influence.
- Developing self-awareness and discipline is critical for long-term trading success.

9.3 Decision-Making Under Uncertainty

Markets are inherently unpredictable. No trader can know the future with certainty, and outcomes are influenced by countless factors — economic reports, geopolitical events, investor sentiment, and random noise. Effective traders recognize that uncertainty is not a weakness to avoid, but a reality to manage.

Understanding Uncertainty in Trading

- **Market Unpredictability:** Even with perfect analysis, trades can fail due to unforeseen events.
- **Probability vs. Certainty:** Trading is about assessing the likelihood of outcomes, not guaranteeing profits.
- **Complex Interactions:** Asset prices are affected by global economic conditions, policy changes, and investor psychology simultaneously.

Tools for Making Decisions Under Uncertainty

- **Probabilistic Thinking:** Evaluate trades by expected value (EV) and probability-weighted outcomes.

- **Scenario Analysis:** Consider multiple outcomes — best-case, worst-case, and most likely scenarios.
- **Position Sizing:** Allocate capital according to the uncertainty and potential risk of each trade.
- **Diversification:** Spread trades across multiple instruments or strategies to reduce overall risk exposure.

Cognitive Strategies

- **Avoid Overconfidence:** Acknowledge that even well-researched trades can fail.
- **Focus on Process, Not Outcome:** Measure success by adherence to your trading plan and probabilistic thinking, not individual wins or losses.
- **Use Checklists:** Reduce errors and emotional bias by confirming each trade meets predefined criteria.
- **Continuous Learning:** Review past trades to identify where assumptions failed or probabilities were misjudged.

Example: Probabilistic Decision in Forex Trading

A trader analyzing EUR/USD sees a 55% chance of the pair rising due to a strong economic report and a 45% chance of decline due to unexpected political news. They calculate the expected value of entering a 1-lot trade:

$$EV = (0.55 \times \$500) + (0.45 \times -\$400) = 275 - 180 = \$95$$

By acknowledging uncertainty and using probability to guide the decision, the trader takes a calculated, rational position rather than guessing.

Key Takeaways

- Markets are uncertain; no trade can be predicted with absolute certainty.
- Successful traders think in probabilities, not guarantees.

- Tools like scenario analysis, position sizing, and diversification help manage uncertainty.
- Cognitive discipline — focusing on process, avoiding overconfidence, and learning from past trades — is essential for long-term success.
- Treat every trade as a probabilistic decision, increasing expected value over time rather than seeking single "sure wins."

Key Takeaways

- **Markets are shaped by human psychology:** Investor behavior, emotions, and biases significantly influence price movements, often creating opportunities and risks.
- **Cognitive biases are common:** Biases like overconfidence, confirmation bias, loss aversion, and anchoring can distort perception and decision-making.
- **Emotional traps can harm trading:** Fear, greed, and panic can lead to impulsive decisions, overtrading, or premature exits.
- **Herd behavior drives trends:** Following the crowd can amplify market movements, creating bubbles or sudden crashes.
- **Decision-making under uncertainty is key:** Accept that no trade is guaranteed; think in probabilities, not certainties.
- **Scenario planning reduces risk:** Considering best-case, worst-case, and most-likely outcomes helps manage uncertainty.
- **Process over outcomes:** Focus on following your trading plan and probabilistic decision-making rather than obsessing over individual wins or losses.
- **Discipline and self-awareness matter:** Keeping a trading journal and regularly reviewing decisions helps identify psychological errors and improve long-term performance.
- **Use structured tools:** Checklists, stop-losses, position sizing, and diversification help counteract biases and emotional influences.

- **Continuous learning is essential:** Studying past trades, market behavior, and your own reactions strengthens both cognitive and emotional trading skills.

Chapter 10

Scenario Planning & Adaptability

Introduction

Markets are rarely static. Prices can surge in a bull market, decline in a bear market, or move sideways for extended periods. Many traders fail because they treat the market as a single, predictable environment rather than a dynamic system that requires constant adaptation.

This chapter focuses on **scenario planning and adaptability** — skills that allow traders to anticipate different market conditions, adjust strategies on the fly, and maintain an edge even when uncertainty is high. By preparing for bull, bear, and sideways markets, and by developing a flexible trading system, you can reduce losses, exploit opportunities, and make your trading approach resilient to change.

10.1 Planning for Bull, Bear, and Sideways Markets

Markets are dynamic and rarely move in a straight line. To succeed as a trader, you must identify the market phase and tailor your strategies accordingly. The three main market types are:

1. **Bull Market:** Prices are generally rising with strong momentum.
2. **Bear Market:** Prices are generally falling with increased volatility.

3. **Sideways Market:** Prices fluctuate within a range with no clear trend.

1. Bull Market Case

Scenario: A major stock index, like the S&P 500, has been trending upward for several months. Economic indicators, corporate earnings, and investor sentiment are positive.

Trader Approach:

- Focus on long positions, trend-following strategies, and breakout trades.
- Use technical tools like moving averages (50-day, 200-day) to confirm trend strength.
- Allocate a portion of capital for pullbacks to optimize entry points.
- Maintain discipline with stop-loss levels to protect gains.

Example Trade: Riya notices Tesla stock breaking above a resistance level with high volume. She enters a long position, sets a trailing stop-loss below recent support, and gradually increases her position as the trend continues.

Key Bull Market Rules:

- Follow the trend; avoid trying to time tops.
- Stick to high-probability setups that align with market momentum.
- Keep some cash ready for buying opportunities during minor corrections.

2. Bear Market Case

Scenario: Economic data points to a slowdown, stock indices decline, and volatility spikes. Investor sentiment turns negative.

Trader Approach:

- Prioritize capital preservation over aggressive gains.
- Reduce exposure to high-beta or cyclical assets.
- Consider hedging strategies such as protective puts or inverse ETFs.
- Limit leverage and monitor stop-loss levels strictly.

Example Trade: Sameer holds a tech-heavy portfolio. Anticipating a market drop, he buys put options on major holdings and shifts part of his portfolio into defensive sectors like utilities and consumer staples.

Key Bear Market Rules:

- Avoid chasing losses; focus on risk control.
- Use hedging tools to mitigate downside.
- Be patient; wait for signs of trend reversal before re-entering aggressively.

3. Sideways Market Case

Scenario: A stock or index trades within a narrow range for weeks. There is no clear uptrend or downtrend.

Trader Approach:

- Trade the range: buy near support, sell near resistance.
- Use oscillators like RSI, Stochastic, or MACD to identify overbought/oversold conditions.
- Keep position sizes small to manage risk in case of sudden breakouts or breakdowns.

Example Trade: Aarav notices Apple stock oscillating between $100 and $110. He buys near $101 (support) and sells near $109 (resistance), repeating this process until a breakout occurs.

Key Sideways Market Rules:

- Range-trading works best; avoid trend-following strategies.
- Focus on precision entries and exits.
- Always monitor for unexpected breakouts and adjust risk management accordingly.

General Guidelines Across All Market Types

- Always define your risk per trade, regardless of the market phase.
- Combine technical analysis, probability assessment, and market context.

- Keep a journal of trades, noting market type, strategy applied, and outcomes.
- Adapt strategies dynamically; a bull market can turn sideways, and a sideways market can break into a trend.

Key Takeaways

- Identifying the market environment is the foundation for successful trading.
- Each market type demands a specific approach: trend-following in bulls, hedging and caution in bears, range-trading in sideways markets.
- Risk management and position sizing remain critical in all conditions.
- Planning and adaptability improve consistency and reduce emotional trading.

10.2 Adapting Your Strategy to Market Changes

Markets are constantly evolving, influenced by economic news, policy decisions, technological innovations, and investor sentiment. A strategy that works in one market phase may fail in another. Successful traders are those who can adapt their approach dynamically rather than sticking rigidly to a single method.

Why Adaptability Matters

Rigid strategies ignore reality. Markets rarely behave exactly as predicted, and external shocks (interest rate changes, geopolitical events, earnings surprises) can render static plans ineffective. Adapting strategies allows traders to:

- Protect capital during unexpected downturns.
- Exploit emerging opportunities in changing market conditions.
- Maintain consistent performance across bull, bear, and sideways markets.

Techniques to Adapt

1. **Re-evaluate Market Conditions Regularly:** Review charts, volatility, and trend indicators weekly to confirm whether the current strategy still aligns with the market.
2. **Adjust Position Sizes:** Reduce exposure when uncertainty increases or when markets are volatile, and increase it cautiously when probability is favorable.
3. **Diversify Approaches:** Maintain multiple strategies (trend-following, mean-reversion, range trading) and select the one that fits the current environment.
4. **Incorporate Probabilistic Thinking:** Continuously assess expected value, win probability, and risk-reward ratios before executing trades.
5. **Use Stop-Losses and Hedging:** Always implement protective measures to minimize losses if the market moves against you unexpectedly.

Practical Example

Riya was using a trend-following strategy on tech stocks during a strong bull market. Suddenly, volatility spiked due to regulatory news affecting the sector. Recognizing the change, she:

- Shifted to smaller positions and tighter stop-losses.
- Focused on high-probability swing trades rather than aggressive trend entries.
- Introduced hedges using options to protect her portfolio.

By adapting, Riya avoided large losses and maintained steady performance, rather than blindly following her original strategy.

Checklist for Adapting Strategies

- Identify if the current market aligns with your strategy.
- Review performance metrics from recent trades.
- Adjust trade size and risk allocation.
- Consider alternative strategies better suited for current conditions.
- Reassess frequently — adaptability is an ongoing process.

Key Takeaways

- No strategy works in all market conditions; flexibility is essential.
- Regular assessment of the market and strategy performance prevents avoidable losses.
- Adjusting trade size, risk, and approach according to the environment enhances long-term consistency.
- A probabilistic mindset complements adaptability, allowing informed decisions in uncertain markets.

10.3 Developing a Flexible Trading System

A flexible trading system is designed to thrive in different market conditions while minimizing emotional decision-making. It is not a rigid set of rules that work in only one type of market, but a dynamic framework that adapts to changes in volatility, trend, and liquidity.

Core Principles of Flexibility

- **Modularity:** Your system should consist of interchangeable components—entry rules, exit rules, risk management, and position sizing—that can be adjusted independently.
- **Scenario-Based Rules:** Define separate rules for bull, bear, and sideways markets, so your system automatically adapts depending on the current environment.
- **Risk Control:** Include built-in risk limits for each strategy and instrument to prevent catastrophic losses if market conditions shift.
- **Continuous Feedback Loop:** Regularly review performance metrics and market conditions to tweak rules and indicators as needed.

Steps to Build a Flexible System

1. **Identify Market Conditions:** Use indicators, trend analysis, and volatility measures to classify the current market as bullish, bearish, or sideways.

2. **Select Strategy Modules:** Choose strategies suited for the current market type. For example, trend-following for bull markets, range trading for sideways markets, and defensive or hedging strategies for bear markets.

3. **Define Entry and Exit Rules:** For each strategy, set clear conditions for entering and exiting trades. Include stop-loss, take-profit, and trailing stop mechanisms.

4. **Incorporate Position Sizing:** Adjust position sizes based on risk appetite, volatility, and probability of success.

5. **Integrate Probabilistic Assessment:** Evaluate expected value, risk-reward, and win probability for each trade. Only take trades that meet your probabilistic threshold.

6. **Backtest and Paper Trade:** Simulate your system on historical data and demo accounts to validate performance under different market scenarios.

7. **Iterate and Refine:** Use results and market feedback to adjust rules, indicators, and modules. Flexibility is not static—it evolves with market conditions.

Practical Example

Kabir built a flexible system with three modules:

- **Bull Market Module:** Trend-following strategy using moving averages and breakouts.

- **Sideways Market Module:** Range-trading using support and resistance zones with oscillators like RSI.

- **Bear Market Module:** Hedging strategies and short-selling with tight stop-loss rules.

Each week, he evaluated market conditions. When the S&P 500 shifted from bullish to sideways, he switched from trend-following to range trading without changing the overall risk profile of his portfolio. This system allowed him to maintain consistent performance and control losses during unexpected market changes.

Checklist for Developing a Flexible Trading System

- Identify market condition types (bull, bear, sideways).
- Define separate strategy modules for each condition.
- Establish entry, exit, and risk management rules for each module.
- Integrate position sizing and probabilistic decision-making.
- Regularly backtest and paper trade new or adjusted modules.
- Review performance and refine the system periodically.

Key Takeaways

- Flexibility is essential for long-term trading success.
- Modular systems allow you to adapt strategies without overhauling your entire approach.
- Probabilistic thinking, proper risk management, and scenario planning make the system robust across market conditions.
- Continuous iteration, backtesting, and learning are required to keep the system effective.

Key Takeaways

- **Plan for all market scenarios:** Always have strategies prepared for bull, bear, and sideways markets to reduce emotional decision-making.
- **Market awareness:** Continuously monitor market conditions and adjust your approach according to trends, volatility, and news events.
- **Flexible systems:** Break your trading system into modular components—entry, exit, risk management, position sizing—that can be adapted as markets change.
- **Scenario-specific tactics:**
  - Bull markets: Focus on trend-following strategies and ride momentum.

  - Bear markets: Protect capital, use hedging or shorting strategies, and reduce risk exposure.
  - Sideways markets: Emphasize range trading, mean-reversion, and avoid overleveraging.

- **Probabilistic thinking:** Evaluate expected value, risk-reward, and probability of outcomes before taking trades in any scenario.
- **Iterative improvement:** Regularly review your trades, backtest strategies, and refine your system to stay aligned with changing market conditions.
- **Risk management integration:** Protective measures and position sizing should be scenario-aware to limit losses and maximize opportunity.
- **Long-term adaptability:** A trader's edge comes from the ability to evolve with markets while maintaining discipline and a probabilistic mindset.

Part IV

Strategies

Chapter 11

Simple Strategies for Beginners

Introduction

Entering the trading world can be overwhelming for beginners. Charts, indicators, and news all compete for attention, making it easy to get lost in the noise.

This chapter focuses on **simple, high-probability strategies** that help beginners understand market behavior, build confidence, and practice discipline. By mastering these foundational techniques, traders can develop the skills and mindset required to progress to more advanced strategies with lower risk.

A Story: First Steps in Strategy

Aarav, a beginner trader, wanted to make consistent profits but didn't know where to start. He tried random trades and lost money initially. His mentor advised: "Start with simple strategies, understand patterns, and manage risk before moving to advanced techniques." This chapter focuses on beginner-friendly strategies that help build confidence and understanding of market dynamics.

11.1 Trend Following

Trend following is one of the most widely used and time-tested trading strategies. The core principle is simple: *"The trend is your friend."* Traders using this approach aim to enter positions in the direction of an established market trend and ride it until signs of a reversal appear.

Understanding Trends

A trend is the general direction in which an asset's price is moving over time. Trends can be:

- **Uptrend:** Higher highs and higher lows. Indicates bullish market sentiment.
- **Downtrend:** Lower highs and lower lows. Indicates bearish market sentiment.
- **Sideways/Range-bound:** Price moves within a horizontal range. Trend following is less effective in this scenario.

Key Tools for Trend Following

Trend following relies on a combination of technical indicators, chart analysis, and price action. Common tools include:

- **Moving Averages (SMA, EMA):** Help identify the direction of the trend and potential support/resistance levels.
- **Trend Lines:** Connect consecutive highs or lows to visualize the trend.
- **ADX (Average Directional Index):** Measures trend strength.
- **Price Patterns:** Breakouts, higher highs, and lower lows signal trend continuation.

Entry and Exit Rules

Entry: Traders typically enter after confirmation of a trend:

- Buy when price is above a rising moving average.
- Sell/short when price is below a declining moving average.
- Confirm trend using volume or momentum indicators.

Exit: Knowing when to exit is crucial to preserving profits:

- Exit when price closes below a key moving average in an uptrend.
- Use trailing stops to capture gains while allowing the trend to continue.
- Take profits at pre-defined resistance/support levels or based on risk-reward ratios.

Risk Management

Trend following can produce large profits, but risk management is essential:

- Always set stop-loss orders to limit losses if the trend reverses unexpectedly.
- Avoid over-leveraging; the market can move against the trend quickly.
- Only risk a small percentage of trading capital on any single trade.

Example: Trend Following in Action

Suppose a trader identifies an uptrend in Apple stock:

- Price is above the 50-day EMA and forming higher highs.
- Trader enters at $150 with a stop-loss at $145.
- Price rises to $165. The trader trails the stop to $160 to lock in profits.

The trader captures a significant portion of the trend while controlling risk.

Key Takeaways

- Trend following is about aligning with the market momentum rather than predicting reversals.
- Patience and discipline are critical — trends take time to develop.
- Combining trend indicators, price action, and proper risk management improves the probability of success.
- This strategy works best in markets that exhibit clear, sustained trends and can be less effective in choppy or sideways markets.

11.2 Breakout Trading

Breakout trading is a strategy that focuses on entering a trade when the price moves beyond a defined support or resistance level. The idea is to capture the momentum as the price "breaks out" of a consolidation or range.

Understanding Breakouts

A breakout occurs when the price moves decisively above resistance or below support:

- **Bullish Breakout:** Price rises above a resistance level, signaling potential upward momentum.
- **Bearish Breakout:** Price falls below a support level, signaling potential downward momentum.
- **False Breakout:** The price temporarily crosses a level but quickly reverses, requiring careful validation.

Identifying Key Levels

To trade breakouts successfully, traders identify significant support and resistance:

- Horizontal levels where price repeatedly reverses.
- Trend lines that connect highs or lows.
- Moving averages acting as dynamic support/resistance.
- Psychological levels (e.g., round numbers like $50 or $100).

Entry Rules

- Enter a long trade when price closes above resistance with increased volume.
- Enter a short trade when price closes below support with increased volume.
- Confirm the breakout using indicators such as RSI, MACD, or Bollinger Bands to avoid false signals.

Exit and Risk Management

- Place stop-loss slightly below the breakout level (for longs) or above it (for shorts).
- Set profit targets based on previous range size, risk-reward ratio, or key technical levels.
- Avoid overleveraging; false breakouts can trigger quick losses.
- Use trailing stops to lock in profits if the breakout continues strongly.

Example: Trading a Bullish Breakout

Suppose a stock has been trading between \$100 (support) and \$110 (resistance) for several weeks:

- Price closes above \$110 with higher volume.
- Trader enters a long position at \$111 with a stop-loss at \$108.
- Target profit is set at \$120, based on the height of the previous range.

Key Takeaways

- Breakout trading aims to capture momentum after the price breaches key levels.
- Confirmation with volume and technical indicators helps reduce the risk of false breakouts.
- Proper risk management, stop-loss placement, and profit targets are crucial for consistent success.
- Patience is essential; not every potential breakout should be traded.

11.3 Swing Trading Basics

Swing trading is a medium-term trading strategy that aims to capture price "swings" within a trend. Unlike day trading, positions are held for several days to weeks, allowing traders to benefit from both short-term momentum and broader trends.

Core Principles

- **Trend Identification:** Recognize whether the market is in an uptrend, downtrend, or range-bound.
- **Entry Timing:** Enter trades near support in an uptrend or resistance in a downtrend.
- **Exit Strategy:** Set clear profit targets and stop-loss levels to protect capital.
- **Risk Management:** Typically risk 1–2% of capital per trade.

Tools for Swing Trading

- Technical indicators like Moving Averages, RSI, MACD.
- Chart patterns such as flags, triangles, and head & shoulders.
- Candlestick analysis to identify reversal or continuation signals.

Example: Swing Trade in Action

Suppose a stock is in an uptrend:

- The stock pulls back to a support level at $50.
- RSI indicates the stock is oversold, signaling a potential bounce.
- Enter a long position at $50, place a stop-loss at $48, and target $56 based on previous highs.

Advantages of Swing Trading

- Captures larger price moves than intraday trading.
- Requires less screen time than day trading.
- Allows for careful analysis and disciplined decision-making.

Disadvantages

- Exposure to overnight and weekend risk.
- Requires patience; trades may take days or weeks to reach targets.

Key Takeaways

- Swing trading balances risk and reward by capturing medium-term price movements.
- Effective strategy combines trend analysis, technical indicators, and disciplined risk management.
- Keeping a trading journal helps refine entries, exits, and overall performance.

Mini Case Study: 3 Beginner Trades Explained

To illustrate beginner-friendly strategies, let's examine three trades executed by a novice trader, Aarav. Each trade focuses on a different type of strategy: trend following, breakout, and swing trading.

Trade 1: Trend Following

- **Asset:** Apple Inc. (AAPL)
- **Strategy:** Buy during an established uptrend using a 20-day SMA for trend confirmation.
- **Entry:** $170 when the stock bounced off the 20-day SMA.
- **Exit:** $180 after 10 days when the stock showed signs of slowing momentum.
- **Outcome:** Profit $10 per share.

Trade 2: Breakout Trading

- **Asset:** EUR/USD Forex pair
- **Strategy:** Enter trades when price breaks a consolidation range.
- **Entry:** 1.1000 after the pair broke above resistance at 1.0980.
- **Exit:** 1.1070 with a stop-loss at 1.0970.
- **Outcome:** Captured 70 pips.

Trade 3: Swing Trading

- **Asset:** Tesla Inc. (TSLA)
- **Strategy:** Buy on short-term pullbacks within a larger trend.
- **Entry:** $750 when price touched a support trendline and RSI was oversold.
- **Exit:** $800 after 1 week as the stock rebounded.
- **Outcome:** Profit $50 per share.

Key Lessons

- Stick to one strategy per trade until comfortable.
- Use technical signals and risk management to guide entries and exits.
- Document every trade in a journal to identify patterns, mistakes, and areas for improvement.

Exercise: Execute a Demo Swing Trade

Swing trading focuses on capturing short- to medium-term price movements within an overall trend. This exercise will help you practice strategy execution without risking real money.

Step 1: Choose an Asset

Select a stock, forex pair, or cryptocurrency that has visible swings over the past few weeks. For example:

- Stock: Tesla (TSLA), Apple (AAPL)
- Forex: EUR/USD, GBP/USD
- Crypto: Bitcoin (BTC), Ethereum (ETH)

Step 2: Analyze the Chart

- Identify support and resistance levels.
- Look for short-term pullbacks or consolidations within a larger trend.

- Note key indicators like RSI or MACD to confirm potential entry points.

Step 3: Set Up the Trade in a Demo Account

- Determine entry price, stop-loss, and target exit price.
- Use realistic position sizing based on your demo account balance.
- Record your plan in a trading journal.

Step 4: Monitor the Trade

- Observe price movements and note any deviations from your plan.
- Practice patience and avoid impulsive decisions.
- Track trade performance in your journal.

Step 5: Review and Learn

- Compare your planned entry/exit with actual results.
- Reflect on your decision-making and emotional responses.
- Adjust strategy and plan for future trades based on lessons learned.

Tip: Repeat this exercise multiple times with different assets to gain confidence and identify which swing trading style suits you best.

Key Takeaways

- **Start Simple:** Focus on a few beginner-friendly strategies before exploring advanced techniques. Complexity can overwhelm and lead to mistakes.
- **Trend Following:** Understanding and riding market trends helps capture sustained moves with lower stress than counter-trend trading.
- **Breakout Trading:** Identify key support and resistance levels to exploit sudden price movements. Patience and confirmation are critical.

- **Swing Trading:** A medium-term strategy that balances short-term trading and investing. Use charts, indicators, and stop-losses to manage risk.
- **Demo Accounts Are Essential:** Practice strategies in a risk-free environment before using real capital.
- **Trading Journal:** Recording trades, entry/exit points, and emotional responses builds discipline, self-awareness, and improves decision-making.
- **Risk Management:** Always define stop-loss and position size, even in demo trades, to cultivate proper risk habits.
- **Consistency Over Frequency:** Focus on executing your strategy correctly rather than trading frequently. Quality trades matter more than quantity.
- **Review and Learn:** Evaluate each trade, identify mistakes and successes, and adjust strategies accordingly.

Chapter 12

Advanced Trading Strategies

Introduction

As traders gain experience, they often seek strategies that go beyond basic trend-following or swing trades. Advanced strategies provide tools to manage risk more effectively, exploit complex market scenarios, and increase potential returns.

This chapter explores techniques like options and derivatives, algorithmic trading, hedging, and arbitrage. Each approach comes with its own set of requirements, challenges, and opportunities. Understanding them is key to evolving from a beginner to a professional-level trader.

By the end of this chapter, you will know not only how these strategies work, but also when and why to apply them.

A Story: Stepping Up to Advanced Techniques

Kabir had mastered beginner strategies and wanted to reduce risk while seeking higher returns. He discovered advanced strategies that allow traders to leverage derivatives, automate trades, and hedge positions. These tools are powerful but require discipline and understanding.

12.1 Options & Derivatives: Calls, Puts, Spreads

Derivatives are financial instruments whose value derives from an underlying asset, such as a stock, commodity, currency, or index. They allow traders to speculate on price movements, hedge existing positions, or generate income. Among derivatives, options are one of the most widely used due to their flexibility and defined risk.

Call Options

- **Definition:** A call option gives its holder the *right, but not the obligation*, to buy an underlying asset at a predetermined price (strike price) before or on a specific date (expiration date).
- **When to Use:** Buy calls if you expect the price of the underlying asset to rise.
- **Components:**
  - *Strike Price:* The price at which you can buy the asset.
  - *Premium:* The cost of purchasing the option.
  - *Expiration Date:* The last date the option can be exercised.
- **Example:** You buy a call option on Tesla with a $400 strike price expiring in 1 month. Tesla rises to $450. You can buy at $400 and potentially sell at $450. Your profit is the difference minus the premium paid.

Put Options

- **Definition:** A put option gives the holder the *right, but not the obligation*, to sell the underlying asset at a specific strike price before expiration.
- **When to Use:** Buy puts if you expect the asset price to fall.
- **Example:** You purchase a put on Apple at $150 strike price. Apple drops to $130. You can sell at $150, capturing the difference (minus the premium) as profit.

Option Spreads

- **Definition:** Spreads involve buying and selling options of the same type (calls or puts) simultaneously but with different strike prices or expiration dates.
- **Purpose:** Spreads reduce risk, lower cost, and allow traders to profit in specific price ranges.
- **Common Types:**
  - *Vertical Spread:* Buy and sell options with different strike prices but same expiration.
  - *Horizontal/Calendar Spread:* Buy and sell options with the same strike price but different expirations.
- **Example:** Buy a call at $100 and sell a call at $110. If the stock ends at $105, you profit partially; maximum profit occurs at $110. Loss is limited to the net premium paid.

Advanced Considerations

- **Leverage:** Options allow control of a large position with relatively small capital.
- **Time Decay (Theta):** Options lose value as they approach expiration if the underlying does not move favorably.
- **Volatility (Vega):** Options prices increase when market volatility rises, giving traders opportunities even in sideways markets.
- **Hedging:** Options can protect portfolios from adverse price moves.

Practical Tips

- Always consider the premium versus potential payoff.
- Understand your risk: some strategies (like naked calls) can expose you to unlimited loss.
- Use spreads to limit risk while still gaining from directional moves.
- Paper trade options first to understand mechanics before using real capital.

Key Takeaways

- Calls = bullish, puts = bearish, spreads = controlled-risk strategies.
- Options provide leverage, but risk management is critical.
- Understanding Greeks (Delta, Theta, Vega, Gamma) helps quantify sensitivity to price, time, and volatility.
- Mastery of options enables traders to speculate, hedge, and implement advanced strategies with defined risk.

12.2 Algorithmic & Quantitative Trading

In modern markets, speed, precision, and data-driven decisions are critical. **Algorithmic trading** and **quantitative trading** combine technology, mathematics, and statistics to give traders an edge. These strategies automate trade execution and identify patterns that may not be visible to the human eye.

Algorithmic Trading

Algorithmic trading uses computer programs to automatically execute trades based on pre-defined rules.

- **Definition:** A method of placing orders automatically when certain market conditions are met.
- **Key Components:**
  - Entry and exit rules
  - Position sizing and risk management
  - Execution algorithms for speed and efficiency
- **Example:** A bot is programmed to buy EUR/USD if the price rises above the 50-day moving average and sell if it falls below, with automatic stop-loss placement.
- **Benefits:** Rapid execution, emotion-free trading, and the ability to operate 24/7.

Quantitative Trading

Quantitative trading involves strategies based on mathematical models and statistical analysis.

- **Definition:** Trading decisions derived from analyzing historical data and measurable factors.
- **Key Techniques:**
  - Statistical arbitrage: exploiting price differences between related assets
  - Momentum and mean-reversion strategies
  - Factor-based investing: selecting assets based on metrics such as growth, value, or volatility
- **Example:** Using historical price data, a quant model finds that stocks showing strong short-term momentum often continue rising the following week. The algorithm automatically buys these stocks and exits according to risk rules.

Tools & Platforms

- Programming languages: Python, R, MATLAB for analysis and model building
- Broker APIs: Interactive Brokers, Alpaca, Binance, etc. for automated trade execution
- Backtesting frameworks: Simulate strategies on historical data to validate performance before live deployment

Risks and Considerations

- Model risk: Past performance may not predict future outcomes
- Overfitting: A model may work perfectly on historical data but fail in live conditions
- Infrastructure risk: Reliable internet, servers, and low-latency execution are essential
- Regulatory compliance: Strategies must follow exchange and legal rules

Key Takeaways

- Algorithmic trading automates execution; quantitative trading relies on data-driven decision-making.
- Both approaches reduce emotional bias but introduce technical and model risks.
- Continuous monitoring, rigorous backtesting, and sound risk management are crucial.
- A strong understanding of programming, statistics, and market behavior is necessary to succeed.

12.3 Hedging, Pairs Trading, Arbitrage

Advanced traders often seek ways to manage risk and exploit market inefficiencies. This section explains three key techniques used by professionals to protect capital and generate profits in different market conditions.

1. Hedging

- **Definition:** A strategy to reduce or offset potential losses in an investment by taking an opposite position in a related asset.
- **Purpose:** Protect your portfolio from adverse market movements.
- **Example:**
  - You own 100 shares of Apple. Fearing a short-term decline, you buy put options on Apple, giving you the right to sell at a predetermined price. If the stock falls, losses on the shares are partially offset by gains on the puts.
- **Key Tip:** Hedging reduces risk but may also reduce potential profits.

2. Pairs Trading

- **Definition:** A market-neutral strategy involving two correlated assets. You go long on the underperforming asset and short the outperforming one.

- **Purpose:** Profit from the relative movement between two assets regardless of overall market direction.
- **Example:**
  - Stock A and Stock B are historically correlated. Stock A underperforms while Stock B rises. You buy Stock A and short Stock B, anticipating the spread will revert to its historical average.
- **Key Tip:** Requires careful correlation analysis and monitoring.

3. Arbitrage

- **Definition:** Exploiting price differences of the same or similar asset in different markets to earn a risk-free profit.
- **Types:**
  - **Spatial Arbitrage:** Buy in one market, sell in another at a higher price.
  - **Triangular Forex Arbitrage:** Exploit discrepancies among three currency pairs.
  - **Statistical Arbitrage:** Use quantitative models to identify mispricings between assets.
- **Example:** Bitcoin trades at $30,000 on Exchange A and $30,200 on Exchange B. Buying on A and selling on B yields a near risk-free profit.

Key Takeaways

- Hedging protects against downside but may limit gains.
- Pairs trading profits from relative movements, not market direction.
- Arbitrage exploits pricing inefficiencies and requires speed and precision.
- All three strategies need strong analysis, risk control, and monitoring.

Exercise: Paper-Trade 1 Hedged vs 1 Unhedged Position

Objective: Understand the difference in risk and reward between hedged and unhedged trades.

1. Choose a financial instrument (e.g., a currency pair, stock, or commodity).
2. Open two simulated trades:
   - **Unhedged Position:** Go long or short without any protection.
   - **Hedged Position:** Apply a hedge using options, futures, or correlated assets to limit downside risk.
3. Track both positions over a period (1–2 weeks recommended) in a trading journal. Record:
   - Entry and exit prices
   - Daily profit/loss
   - Risk exposure
   - Emotional response to market moves
4. Compare outcomes:
   - How did the hedge affect losses during adverse price moves?
   - How did profits differ between the hedged and unhedged positions?
5. Reflect on the trade: Did hedging reduce stress and risk? Did it limit gains?

Key Takeaway: Practicing hedged vs unhedged trades helps build intuition on risk management, shows the trade-offs of protection, and prepares you for real-world trading decisions.

Key Takeaways

- **Advanced strategies** help traders manage risk, enhance returns, and exploit complex market opportunities.

- **Options and derivatives** (calls, puts, spreads) are powerful tools for hedging, speculation, and income generation.
- **Algorithmic and quantitative trading** uses rules, models, and automation to remove emotion and exploit statistical edges.
- **Hedging, pairs trading, and arbitrage** reduce exposure to unwanted risks and can generate consistent profits under the right conditions.
- **Practical application is critical:** Paper trading hedged vs unhedged positions allows learning without real capital at risk.
- **Discipline, analysis, and preparation** remain the foundation of successful advanced trading.

Chapter 13

Position Sizing & Risk Management

Introduction

Success in trading is not just about picking winning trades — it's about managing losses and protecting capital. Position sizing and risk management determine how much of your portfolio is exposed to any single trade, helping prevent catastrophic losses. By mastering these concepts, traders can survive losing streaks, trade with confidence, and ensure that profits compound over time. This chapter will guide you through practical methods to size positions, set stop losses, and manage overall portfolio risk.

A Story: Protecting Capital

Meera was making winning trades but noticed that a single loss wiped out a large portion of her profits. She realized that without proper position sizing and risk management, even good strategies could fail. This chapter focuses on controlling risk and preserving capital — the most important skill for any trader.

13.1 Risk per Trade (1–2% Rule)

One of the most important principles in trading is **controlling risk per trade**. Many successful traders adhere to the **1–2% rule**, which means that you should never risk more than 1–2% of your total trading capital on a single trade. This simple rule is a cornerstone of capital preservation and long-term profitability.

Why Risk Management Matters

Even the most profitable strategy will fail if risk is not controlled. A few consecutive losses with large position sizes can wipe out a trading account. Limiting risk per trade:

- Preserves capital during drawdowns.
- Reduces emotional stress and impulsive decision-making.
- Keeps you in the market long enough for your edge to work.

Calculating Risk per Trade

To determine the correct position size, follow these steps:

1. **Determine your account size:** The total capital you are willing to trade.
2. **Decide your risk percentage:** Typically 1–2% per trade.
3. **Set your stop-loss:** The price level where the trade will automatically close if the market moves against you.
4. **Calculate position size:**

$$PositionSize = \frac{AccountSize \times Risk\%}{EntryPrice - Stop - LossPrice}$$

Example 1: Stock Trade

- Account size: \$10,000
- Risk per trade: 1% (\$100)
- Stock entry: \$50
- Stop-loss: \$48 (\$2 risk per share)

$$PositionSize = \frac{100}{2} = 50shares$$

If the stock hits the stop-loss, the maximum loss is $100, exactly 1% of your account.

Example 2: Forex Trade

- Account size: $20,000
- Risk per trade: 2% ($400)
- Currency pair: EUR/USD
- Stop-loss: 50 pips

$$PositionSize = \frac{400}{50pips} = 8units(orminilots)$$

Even if the stop-loss is hit, the trader only loses 2% of the account.

Advanced Considerations

- **Volatility Adjustment:** Reduce position size in highly volatile markets; increase slightly in stable conditions.
- **Correlation Management:** Avoid risking multiple trades that are highly correlated simultaneously, as this can amplify losses.
- **Portfolio Perspective:** Risk per trade should be considered across all open positions, not individually.
- **Dynamic Adjustment:** As your account grows or shrinks, recalculate the risk per trade continuously.

Common Mistakes to Avoid

- Ignoring stop-loss placement: Risking 2% doesn't help if you set your stop-loss too wide.
- Chasing losses: Increasing position size after a loss violates the rule and can lead to account blow-up.

- Focusing on potential gains instead of risk: Always prioritize preserving capital over chasing high returns.

Key Takeaways

- Limiting risk per trade protects your capital, which is the most valuable asset in trading.
- The 1–2% rule allows you to survive losing streaks while keeping enough capital to take advantage of opportunities.
- Consistently applying this principle builds discipline, reduces emotional trading, and lays the foundation for long-term success.

13.2 Stop Loss & Take Profit Placement

Controlling risk is only part of the equation — knowing exactly where to exit a trade, both when it goes against you and when it goes in your favor, is equally important. Stop loss and take profit orders are tools that help automate these exits, protecting capital and locking in gains.

Stop Loss: Limiting Losses

A **stop loss** is an order to automatically exit a trade at a predetermined price if the market moves against you. Its primary goal is to prevent small losses from turning into account-destroying ones.

- **Purpose:** Protect your trading capital and control risk per trade.
- **Types:**
  - **Fixed Dollar/Percentage Stop:** Exit if loss reaches a specific dollar amount or
  - **Technical Stop:** Placed at key support/resistance levels, moving averages, or trend lines.
  - **Trailing Stop:** Adjusts dynamically as the trade moves in your favor, locking in profits while allowing room to grow.
- **Example:** You buy a stock at $50, and your analysis shows a strong support at $48. Setting a stop loss at $48 limits your potential loss to $2 per share.

Take Profit: Locking Gains

A **take profit** order automatically closes your position when the price reaches a favorable level. It ensures that profits are realized before the market reverses.

- **Purpose:** Avoid letting winners turn into losers due to greed or market reversals.
- **Placement Methods:**
  - **Risk-Reward Ratio:** Place take profit at a multiple of your stop loss (e.g., 2:1, 3:1).
  - **Technical Levels:** Use resistance, previous highs, Fibonacci extensions, or pivot points.
  - **Partial Profits:** Close part of the position at the first target and let the rest run with a trailing stop.
- **Example:** Buy at $50 with a $48 stop loss and a desired 2:1 risk-reward ratio. The take profit would be $54, giving $4 potential gain vs $2 risk.

Best Practices for Placement

- Always set stop loss before entering a trade — never "hope" the market will reverse.
- Align stop loss and take profit with market structure and volatility, not arbitrary numbers.
- Avoid placing stops too tight — you may get stopped out on normal market fluctuations.
- Consider partial exits to lock in gains while giving the trade room to run.
- Use trailing stops to capture larger trends without manually managing every move.

Advanced Tips

- Combine stop loss placement with position sizing to calculate the exact dollar risk.

- Monitor correlations between assets; correlated positions may require adjusting stops to avoid compounded risk.
- Adjust take profit levels based on momentum and news events to capture optimal gains.

Key Takeaways

- Proper stop loss placement protects your capital and enforces discipline.
- Take profit placement ensures consistent gains and removes emotional bias from exits.
- Combining stops, take profits, and position sizing creates a comprehensive risk management framework.

13.3 Portfolio Diversification

One of the oldest and most reliable principles in finance is: *"Don't put all your eggs in one basket."* Diversification means spreading investments across different assets, sectors, or markets to reduce overall risk. While it cannot eliminate risk completely, diversification helps ensure that no single trade or asset failure can destroy your portfolio.

Why Diversification Matters

Markets are unpredictable. A single company, sector, or currency pair can suffer due to unexpected events — earnings disappointments, regulatory changes, geopolitical conflicts, or economic downturns. By diversifying, traders and investors protect themselves from the negative impact of any one position.

- **Risk Reduction:** If one asset declines, gains in others can balance the loss.
- **Stability:** A diversified portfolio tends to have smoother performance over time.
- **Opportunity:** Exposure to different markets allows traders to capture opportunities across sectors or asset classes.

Types of Diversification

- **Asset Class Diversification:** Spread investments across stocks, bonds, commodities, forex, and cryptocurrencies.
- **Sector Diversification:** Within equities, balance holdings across technology, healthcare, finance, energy, etc.
- **Geographic Diversification:** Invest in different countries or regions to reduce dependence on a single economy.
- **Timeframe Diversification:** Combine long-term investments with short-term trades to balance stability and growth.

Examples of Diversification

- **Poor Diversification:** A trader holds only three tech stocks (Apple, Microsoft, Tesla). If technology underperforms, the whole portfolio suffers.
- **Good Diversification:** A trader holds tech stocks, a pharmaceutical company, government bonds, gold, and exposure to the U.S. dollar. If tech falls, bonds and gold may rise, balancing the portfolio.
- **Global Diversification:** Instead of only U.S. stocks, the trader invests in European equities, Asian markets, and emerging economies to spread geopolitical and economic risks.

Practical Guidelines for Traders

- Avoid over-concentration in one stock, asset class, or region.
- Diversify across both **uncorrelated assets** (e.g., gold vs. equities).
- Use ETFs or index funds if building diversification individually is difficult.
- Rebalance periodically to maintain the intended risk exposure.
- Remember: over-diversification (too many small positions) can dilute returns.

Limitations of Diversification

Diversification is powerful but not a silver bullet. During systemic crises (like the 2008 global financial crisis or COVID-19 market crash), most asset classes may fall together. In such times, diversification reduces but cannot eliminate losses. Hence, risk management tools like stop losses and position sizing remain critical.

Key Takeaways

- Diversification spreads risk and reduces portfolio volatility.
- Balance across asset classes, sectors, and geographies for optimal protection.
- Combine diversification with disciplined risk management for long-term survival.

Exercise: Simulate Portfolio and Trades

Objective: Apply risk management in a hypothetical portfolio.

1. Create a $10,000 demo portfolio.
2. Allocate capital across 5-10 instruments (stocks, crypto, or forex).
3. Define risk per trade (1–2%).
4. Set stop loss and take profit for each trade.
5. Record outcomes over simulated trades and calculate overall portfolio performance.

13.4 Risk–Reward Ratios (2:1, 3:1)

Every trade involves **two possible outcomes**:

- **Win** — your reward (profit)
- **Loss** — your risk (loss)

The **Risk–Reward Ratio (RRR)** measures how much you stand to gain compared to how much you risk.

Formula

$$RRR = \frac{Risk(PotentialLoss)}{Reward(PotentialGain)}$$

Example: If you risk \$100 to gain \$200:

$$RRR = \frac{100}{200} = 1:2$$

Why RRR Matters

A favorable RRR can make trading profitable even with a low win rate. *The principle: your winners must be larger than your losers.*

Probability vs. Risk–Reward

The table below shows the minimum win rate required to break even at different RRRs:

Risk–Reward Ratio	Win Rate Needed
1:1	50%
2:1	33.3%
3:1	25%
4:1	20%
5:1	16.7%

Key takeaway:

- At a 1:1 ratio, you need to win at least 50% of trades to break even.
- At 2:1, only about 33% of trades need to be winners.
- At 3:1, you can be wrong 75% of the time and still make a profit.

Example: 3:1 Ratio in Action

A trader risks \$100 to make \$300. Over 10 trades:

$$3 \times 300 = 900, \quad 7 \times 100 = 700$$

$$NetProfit = 900 - 700 = +200$$

Even with only a 30% win rate, the trader remains profitable.

Guidelines

- Aim for trades with at least a 2:1 reward-to-risk ratio.
- Avoid setups where potential reward is smaller than risk.
- Combine RRR with position sizing and stop-loss rules for stronger protection.

Key Insight

Trading is a probability game. You don't need to be right every time — you need your winners to outweigh your losers consistently.

Exercise: Build a $10,000 Portfolio Simulation

Objective: Practice portfolio construction, position sizing, risk management, and performance measurement by simulating a $10,000 trading/investment portfolio over a chosen period (3–12 months). This exercise teaches allocation thinking, trade sizing, rebalancing, and how to evaluate results objectively.

Overview & Rules

- Start capital: **$10,000** (paper money).
- Timeframe: choose 3, 6, or 12 months for the simulation.
- Instruments: pick **5–12** tradable instruments across asset classes (stocks, ETFs, forex pairs, crypto, bonds, commodities).
- Risk per trade: use the **1–2% rule** (recommended 1% for beginners).
- Transaction costs: include commissions/spread assumptions (e.g., $1 per trade or 0.05% per trade).
- Rebalancing: decide an interval (monthly/quarterly) or rules-based triggers.
- Record everything in a trading journal / spreadsheet.

Step-by-step Instructions

Step 1 — Choose assets and timeframe

- Example 8-instrument portfolio:
  - U.S. Large-cap ETF (e.g., SPY)
  - Tech stock (e.g., AAPL)
  - Growth stock (e.g., TSLA)
  - Gold ETF (GLD)
  - 10Y Treasury ETF (IEF)
  - EUR/USD (FX)
  - Bitcoin (BTC)
  - Cash / Stablecoin (0–5%)
- Simulation period: **6 months** (example).

Step 2 — Decide allocation buckets

- Conservative example (beginner): Stocks 40%, Bonds 25%, Gold 10%, Crypto 5%, Cash 20%.
- Balanced example: Stocks 60%, Bonds 15%, Gold 5%, Crypto 5%, Cash 15%.
- Aggressive example: Stocks 70%, Crypto 10%, Commodities 5%, Cash 15%.

Step 3 — Translate allocation into position sizes

$$PositionValue = Allocation\% \times \$10,000$$

Then calculate number of shares/lots using current price and adjust for transaction costs.

Step 4 — Apply risk-per-trade sizing (for active trades)

1. Choose stop-loss in price terms (technical level or volatility-based).
2. Use the 1% rule: \$10,000 × 1% = \$100 ⇒ maximum loss per trade.
3. Position size (shares) = \$100 / (Entry Price - Stop Price).

Step 5 — Execute simulated trades (paper trading)

- Enter trades in your spreadsheet with: Date, Asset, Entry Price, Stop Price, Position Size, Commission, Target Price(s).
- Update daily/weekly prices and mark-to-market P&L.

Step 6 — Rebalancing rules

- Time-based: rebalance monthly/quarterly to original allocation.
- Threshold-based: rebalance when any asset drifts above 5–10% from target weight.
- Tactical: rebalance based on signals (economic data, valuation, momentum).

Step 7 — Track and record Maintain a table with these columns (spreadsheet-friendly):

Date	Asset	Entry	Size	Stop	Current Price	Realized P&L	Unrealized P&L
2025-09-27	BTC/USD	28000	1.0	27500	28500	500	0

Also track portfolio-level daily/weekly equity.

Performance Metrics to Calculate

Include these standard metrics (add formulas in spreadsheet):

- **Total Return:** $\frac{EndingEquity-StartingEquity}{StartingEquity}$
- **CAGR (if >1 year):** $(\frac{Ending}{Starting})^{1/n}-1$ where n = years
- **Max Drawdown:** largest peak-to-trough decline in equity.
- **Win Rate:** $\frac{NumberofWinningTrades}{TotalTrades}$
- **Average Win / Average Loss**
- **Profit Factor:** $\frac{GrossProfit}{GrossLoss}$
- **Sharpe Ratio (approx):** $\frac{MeanReturn}{-}r_f StdDevofReturns$ (use weekly returns)
- **Expectancy per trade:** $E=(W\times AvgWin)-((1-W)\times AvgLoss)$

Sample Starting Template (table)

Asset	Allocation (%)	Position $	Entry Price	Shares/Lots	Stop Price
SPY	30%	3000	445.00	6.74 ⇒ 6	435.00
AAPL	15%	1500	180.00	8.33 ⇒ 8	174.00
GLD	10%	1000	180.00	5.56 ⇒ 5	174.00
BTC	5%	500	30000	0.0167	27000
IEF	20%	2000	100.00	20	98.00
Cash	20%	2000	—	—	—

Suggested Exercises / Variations

1. **Conservative vs Aggressive:** Run two parallel simulations—one conservative allocation, one aggressive—and compare drawdowns and return/risk.
2. **Active vs Passive:** Simulate a buy-and-hold portfolio vs an active trading portfolio that attempts tactical trades and rebalances monthly.
3. **Stress Test:** Apply a 20% market drop mid-simulation to see how your portfolio behaves.
4. **Transaction Cost Sensitivity:** Re-run with higher/lower commissions to quantify impact.
5. **Monte Carlo Walk (optional advanced):** Randomize sequence of returns from your historical trades to see distribution of outcomes.

Reflection Questions (write answers in your journal)

- Which allocation produced the best risk-adjusted return?
- What was the maximum drawdown and how comfortable were you during it?
- Did rebalancing improve results? Which rule worked best?
- Which assets contributed most to returns and which to risk?

- What changes would you implement in a live account?

Deliverables (what to hand in / keep)

- A spreadsheet with daily/weekly marked-to-market portfolio equity.
- Trade log with entries/exits, position sizing, stops, and P&L.
- Summary page with Total Return, Max Drawdown, Win Rate, Profit Factor, Sharpe (weekly), Expectancy.
- Short report (1–2 pages) answering reflection questions and listing lessons learned.

Tips & Best Practices

- Use realistic slippage and commissions—simulations without costs overestimate performance.
- Keep your rules objective: entry, stop, position sizing, and exit should be specified before each trade.
- Update the simulation frequently (daily/weekly) and review performance monthly.
- Treat the exercise as serious learning—be honest about mistakes and document them.

Good luck. This exercise will give you a practical, hands-on understanding of portfolio construction, sizing, and the trade-offs between return and risk. Save your work — your simulation becomes the baseline for improving real trading decisions.

Key Takeaways

- Proper portfolio construction is essential for managing risk and maximizing long-term returns.
- Position sizing, risk per trade, and stop-loss placement are critical components to protect capital.

- Diversification across asset classes and instruments reduces the impact of individual losses.
- Paper trading a simulated portfolio allows for practice without risking real capital.
- Tracking performance metrics (total return, drawdown, Sharpe ratio, profit factor) helps evaluate strategy effectiveness.
- Rebalancing strategies, whether time-based, threshold-based, or tactical, can improve risk-adjusted returns.
- Reflecting on trade outcomes and journaling lessons enhances discipline and decision-making for real trading.

Part V

The Trader's Mindset

Chapter 14

Psychology of Trading

Introduction

Trading is not just about charts, indicators, or strategies — it is fundamentally a mental game. Emotions like fear, greed, impatience, and overconfidence can sabotage even the best-planned trades.

This chapter explores the psychological aspects of trading, including common emotional traps, cognitive biases, and techniques to develop discipline and consistency. By understanding the mind behind the trades, traders can make more rational decisions, stick to their plans, and improve long-term performance.

A Story: Mastering the Mind

Nina was an intelligent trader but often let emotions dictate her trades. She would chase winning trades out of greed and panic-sell during minor losses. Over time, she learned that mastering her mind was as important as mastering strategies.

14.1 Fear, Greed, and Emotional Traps

Trading is as much a psychological challenge as it is a technical one. While charts, indicators, and strategies are important, a trader's success ultimately depends on how well they manage their mind. Emotions like fear and greed can subtly influence decisions, often leading to costly mistakes if left unchecked.

Understanding these emotional traps, recognizing them in real-time, and having tools to manage them are essential for long-term profitability.

1. Common Emotional Traps

Fear of Losing (Loss Aversion): Humans naturally feel losses more strongly than gains of the same size. In trading, this can cause hesitation to enter a high-probability trade or exiting winning trades too early.
Example: A trader sees a stock setup with strong bullish signals but hesitates to buy because of a previous small loss, missing a profitable opportunity.

Greed and Overtrading: The desire for large, quick profits can lead to taking trades that are outside your plan or sizing positions too large.
Example: After two consecutive winning trades, a trader doubles the position size, resulting in a significant loss on the next trade.

Revenge Trading: Attempting to recover from a loss impulsively, often with larger trades and higher risk.
Example: A trader loses $500 on one trade and immediately enters a new trade with double the size, ignoring the strategy rules.

Herd Mentality (Following the Crowd): Entering trades because "everyone else is doing it," rather than based on analysis.
Example: Buying a cryptocurrency during a hype cycle without understanding fundamentals, leading to being trapped when prices reverse.

Analysis Paralysis: Overanalyzing charts, indicators, or news can lead to missed opportunities or delayed decision-making.
Example: A trader spends hours deciding whether to enter a trade and ultimately misses the optimal entry price.

Fear of Missing Out (FOMO): Acting impulsively due to excitement or hype rather than logic and strategy.
Example: Jumping into a breakout trade after a large price move, only to enter at an exhausted level.

2. Psychological Insights Behind Emotional Traps

Behavioral finance teaches us that humans are not always rational. Biases like overconfidence, loss aversion, confirmation bias, and recency effect play a large role in trading errors. Understanding these cognitive biases allows traders to anticipate and mitigate irrational decision-making.

3. Strategies to Manage Emotions

- **Maintain a Trading Journal:** Record trades along with the reasoning, emotional state, and outcome. Reviewing patterns helps identify recurring emotional mistakes.
- **Predefine Entry and Exit Rules:** Stick to your trading plan and set clear stop-loss and take-profit levels. Reduces impulsive decisions.
- **Use Position Sizing and Risk Management:** Limiting exposure ensures no single trade can create emotional panic or irrational moves.
- **Demo Trading and Small Positions:** Build confidence and experience without risking significant capital.
- **Mindfulness and Breaks:** Take regular breaks, practice breathing exercises, and avoid overtrading during stress or fatigue.
- **Review and Adjust:** Weekly reflection on trades and emotional triggers strengthens self-awareness and discipline.

4. Practical Exercise

Exercise: Emotional Awareness Journal For one week, record the following for every trade:

- Emotional state before entry (e.g., anxious, confident, fearful, excited)
- Decision rationale (technical, fundamental, or impulsive)
- Outcome and deviation from plan
- Lessons learned

Review at the end of the week to identify patterns and design strategies to counter emotional traps.

5. Key Takeaways

- Trading success is heavily influenced by psychology; emotions can either make or break your results.
- Fear, greed, FOMO, revenge trading, and herd mentality are common traps that every trader faces.

- Maintaining discipline, journaling trades, using position sizing, and following a predefined plan help mitigate emotional risks.
- Awareness and practice allow traders to gradually transform emotional decision-making into rational, strategy-driven execution.

14.2 Building Discipline & Consistency

Success in trading is not determined solely by strategies or indicators — it is earned through discipline and consistent execution. Many traders fail not because they lack knowledge, but because they cannot stick to a plan, let emotions dictate decisions, or maintain routines that support long-term growth.

1. The Importance of Discipline

Discipline ensures that you follow your trading rules regardless of market noise, peer pressure, or emotional impulses. Without discipline, even a profitable strategy can become a losing one.

Example: A trader identifies a high-probability setup but hesitates because of fear. By sticking to a predefined entry and exit plan, disciplined traders can execute trades consistently, reducing emotional errors.

2. Building Consistency Through Routine

Consistency is achieved by creating structured routines and habits:

- **Daily Review:** Begin each trading day reviewing previous trades, market news, and upcoming economic events.
- **Predefined Trading Plan:** Document entry, exit, position size, and risk per trade. Following this plan builds repeatable habits.
- **End-of-Day Reflection:** Record trades, emotional states, mistakes, and lessons in a trading journal.
- **Scheduled Learning:** Dedicate time to study charts, indicators, and market behavior, even on non-trading days.

3. Overcoming Common Pitfalls

- **Chasing Losses:** Avoid entering trades impulsively to recover from previous losses. Stick to your risk management rules.
- **Overtrading:** Limit the number of trades per day or week to maintain quality over quantity.
- **Deviation from Plan:** Never change your strategy mid-trade based on fear or greed.

4. Practical Exercises

Exercise 1: Trade Plan Adherence For one week, strictly follow your trading plan. Record any deviations and the reason for each.

Exercise 2: Routine Building Set a consistent schedule for market analysis, trade execution, and journaling. Track adherence for 30 days to solidify the habit.

5. Key Takeaways

- Discipline separates successful traders from those who fail despite good strategies.
- Consistency is built through routines, journaling, and adherence to a well-defined trading plan.
- Avoid emotional trading, overtrading, and impulsive decisions by maintaining habits that reinforce discipline.
- Long-term profitability requires both disciplined execution and consistent reflection on performance.

14.3 Dealing with Losses & Drawdowns

Every trader experiences losses — it's an inevitable part of the game. Even the most skilled traders face drawdowns, periods where the account value declines from its previous peak. How you handle these situations determines long-term success.

1. Understanding Losses

Losses are not failures; they are feedback. Each losing trade provides information about your strategy, risk management, and emotional control. Accepting losses as part of trading helps prevent emotional overreactions.

Example: A trader risks 2% per trade and experiences three consecutive losses. Instead of panicking, they recognize this as a normal statistical outcome and continue executing their plan.

2. Drawdowns Explained

A drawdown is the decline in account equity from a peak to a trough. Large drawdowns can erode confidence and capital, so managing their size is critical.

Key Points:

- Keep individual trade risk within defined limits (e.g., 1–2% per trade).
- Diversify positions to avoid correlation-based losses.
- Use stop-losses to prevent catastrophic drawdowns.

3. Emotional Management During Losses

- **Stay Calm:** Avoid revenge trading to recover losses.
- **Focus on Process, Not Outcome:** Concentrate on executing your strategy correctly.
- **Reflect Objectively:** Review losing trades to extract lessons without self-blame.

4. Practical Techniques to Handle Drawdowns

- **Scaling Down:** Reduce position sizes temporarily during a losing streak.
- **Pause Trading:** Take breaks to reassess strategy and mental state.
- **Use Journals:** Record trades, emotional states, and lessons learned to improve resilience.

5. Example Scenario

Suppose your account equity is $50,000 and you experience a 10% drawdown to $45,000. If your average risk per trade is 2%, it would take approximately 5 successful trades to recover the loss. Planning for drawdowns ensures you stay patient and disciplined during such periods.

6. Key Takeaways

- Losses are part of trading; treat them as learning opportunities.
- Drawdowns test both capital and emotional discipline.
- Proper risk management, journaling, and reflection reduce the psychological impact of losses.
- Maintaining patience and adherence to your trading plan is essential for long-term profitability.

Exercise: Daily Trading Journal with Emotions Column

Keeping a daily trading journal is one of the most effective tools for improving as a trader. This exercise focuses not just on recording trades, but also on capturing emotional states, which are often the hidden drivers of success or failure.

Instructions

1. **Create Your Journal:** Use a spreadsheet, notebook, or digital tool like Notion/Excel.
2. **Record Each Trade:** Include details such as:
    - Date & Time
    - Instrument (Stock, Forex, Crypto)
    - Trade Type (Long/Short)
    - Entry Price, Stop-Loss, Take-Profit
    - Position Size
    - Reason for entering the trade (technical/fundamental/strategy)

3. **Track Outcome:** Record whether the trade was a win or loss and the P&L.

4. **Emotions Column:** Include a column to capture how you felt before, during, and after the trade:
   - Nervous, anxious, confident, greedy, fearful
   - Did emotions influence your decision-making?
   - Were you tempted to deviate from your plan?

5. **Reflection:** At the end of each day or week, review your journal:
   - Identify patterns of emotional behavior
   - Note mistakes or successes linked to mindset
   - Adjust your strategy or risk management if needed

Example Entry

Date	Instrument	Type	Entry	SL	TP	Result	Emotions
2025-09-01	EUR/USD	Long	1.1050	1.1020	1.1100	+50 pips	Nervous at entry, confident after confirmation
2025-09-01	AAPL	Short	170	172	165	-2 pts	Greedy, exited too early

Benefits

- Helps identify emotional biases affecting trades
- Improves discipline and adherence to trading plan
- Provides historical data for reviewing strategy effectiveness

Key Takeaway

Consistently journaling trades along with emotional states allows traders to separate intuition from impulse, recognize patterns in behavior, and make more rational, disciplined decisions over time.

Key Takeaways

- Trading psychology is as important as trading strategy. Mastering emotions can prevent impulsive decisions and reduce losses.
- Fear and greed are the primary emotional traps that influence trader behavior. Awareness of these helps maintain discipline.

- Consistency in routines, adherence to a trading plan, and journaling trades strengthens decision-making over time.
- Losses and drawdowns are inevitable; managing them effectively and learning from them is crucial for long-term success.
- Maintaining a daily trading journal with an emotions column allows traders to identify psychological patterns and biases.
- Reflection and review of both wins and losses foster continuous improvement and a more objective trading mindset.
- Discipline, patience, and self-awareness are core skills that differentiate consistently profitable traders from amateurs.

Chapter 15

Advanced Trading Psychology

Introduction

Mastering trading is not just about strategies, charts, or indicators—it's about mastering the mind. Even the most technically skilled traders can falter when emotions, stress, or cognitive biases interfere with decision-making.

This chapter delves into **advanced psychological techniques** that help traders build mental resilience, achieve peak performance, and maintain discipline under pressure. By understanding mental conditioning, flow states, and emotional mastery, you can consistently make rational, probabilistic decisions and turn trading into a skill rather than a gamble.

15.1 Mental Conditioning & Resilience

Trading is often described as one of the most mentally demanding professions. Unlike other fields where effort and intelligence almost guarantee progress, the markets are uncertain, constantly changing, and often punishing. A trader can do everything "right" and still face losses. This uncertainty creates a unique psychological battlefield where **mental conditioning and resilience** determine long-term survival.

Why Mental Conditioning Matters

Mental conditioning is about training the mind to operate under stress, uncertainty, and risk. It involves developing the ability to:

- Stick to your trading plan when emotions tempt you to deviate.
- Manage setbacks and losses without spiraling into fear or revenge trading.
- Stay disciplined and consistent through winning and losing streaks.

Without conditioning, traders often react impulsively—closing trades too early, holding losers too long, or abandoning systems after a few setbacks. A resilient mindset provides the mental "shock absorbers" to handle these inevitable challenges.

Core Components of Resilience in Trading

Resilience in trading can be cultivated across four key dimensions:

1. **Emotional Resilience:** The ability to absorb losses without emotional breakdown. For example, accepting that losing 40% of your trades can still result in profitability if your risk/reward ratio is strong.
2. **Cognitive Resilience:** The flexibility to adapt your thinking, analyze mistakes, and revise strategies rather than rigidly sticking to failing methods.
3. **Behavioral Resilience:** Consistently following your rules and routines—journaling trades, reviewing performance, and sticking to checklists—even under pressure.
4. **Social Resilience:** Building supportive networks—mentors, trading communities, or accountability partners—to share experiences and avoid isolation.

Practical Mental Conditioning Techniques

To strengthen mental resilience, traders can apply practices from sports psychology, performance science, and mindfulness:

- **Pre-Trade Rituals:** Begin each trading session with a routine (reviewing journal notes, setting stop-loss levels, affirming rules). Rituals create consistency and reduce emotional variability.

- **Stress Rehearsal:** Simulate difficult scenarios—large drawdowns, losing streaks, volatile markets—and visualize how you will respond. This builds psychological preparedness.
- **Micro-Recovery:** Short breaks, breathing exercises, or walks during trading help reset focus and prevent decision fatigue.
- **Self-Talk and Affirmations:** Replace negative thoughts ("I can't afford another loss") with constructive framing ("Losses are part of my edge; I will focus on execution").
- **Post-Trade Review:** Regularly debrief after trades, focusing not just on outcomes but on whether you followed your process. This strengthens learning and detaches self-worth from results.

Case Example: The Resilient Trader

Consider a trader who loses five trades in a row. An unconditioned trader might abandon their system or double down recklessly. A resilient trader, however, reviews their journal, confirms that rules were followed, and reminds themselves that probability plays out over many trades, not a few. By staying disciplined, they protect both capital and confidence.

Key Takeaways

- Mental conditioning is as critical as strategy—it determines consistency under stress.
- Resilience spans emotional, cognitive, behavioral, and social dimensions.
- Techniques like rituals, stress rehearsal, micro-recovery, and journaling build mental toughness.
- A resilient trader accepts losses as part of the game and focuses on process, not just outcomes.

15.2 Flow State and Peak Performance

Trading at the highest level is not just about skill, knowledge, or discipline—it is also about achieving the right **mental state**. Psychologists call this the *flow state*: a condition of deep concentration and effortless performance where time seems to slow down, distractions fade, and execution feels natural. Many athletes, musicians, and performers describe flow as being "in the zone." For traders, flow can mean entering and exiting trades with precision, analyzing data with clarity, and making decisions without hesitation or fear.

What is Flow in Trading?

Flow occurs when your skill level is matched to the challenge in front of you. Too little challenge, and you feel bored; too much challenge, and you feel anxious. Flow sits in the middle:

- **High Skill + High Challenge = Flow.**
- **Low Skill + High Challenge = Anxiety.**
- **High Skill + Low Challenge = Boredom.**

In trading, flow is achieved when you have prepared thoroughly (analysis, risk management, rules) and are faced with market conditions that demand your full attention but remain within your ability to handle.

Characteristics of Flow State

According to performance psychology, traders in flow often report:

- Intense, focused concentration on the present moment.
- A merging of action and awareness—trading decisions feel fluid and automatic.
- A loss of self-consciousness; ego and fear fade into the background.
- Distorted sense of time—minutes can feel like seconds.
- Intrinsic enjoyment of the activity itself, regardless of outcome.

Conditions for Entering Flow

While flow cannot be forced, traders can create conditions that make it more likely to occur:

1. **Clear Goals:** Define specific trading objectives for each session (e.g., "I will take only setups that match my system, no more than 2 trades per day").

2. **Immediate Feedback:** Use tools such as trade journaling, P&L dashboards, and risk alerts to know instantly if you're aligned with your plan.

3. **Balanced Challenge:** Trade in markets that match your skill level. A beginner overwhelmed by leveraged crypto futures won't enter flow—they'll enter panic.

4. **Deep Focus Environment:** Eliminate distractions—notifications, noise, multitasking—so your full attention is on the market.

Peak Performance in Trading

Flow is closely tied to peak performance. Athletes reach personal bests when in flow; traders can do the same. But sustaining peak performance requires more than occasional flow—it requires:

- **Preparation:** Reviewing market conditions, rehearsing scenarios, and setting risk parameters before trading.

- **Routine:** Consistent habits that prime the brain for focused work (e.g., starting every session with analysis and meditation).

- **Energy Management:** Proper sleep, nutrition, and exercise, since cognitive energy is the foundation of focus.

- **Recovery:** Regular breaks, days off, and time for reflection to prevent burnout.

Case Example: Flow in Action

Imagine a trader who has prepared all week for a central bank interest rate announcement. They have mapped out scenarios, placed alerts, and defined entry/exit rules. As the market reacts, they execute flawlessly—no hesitation, no panic, just calm precision. Later, they realize hours have passed, but their mind felt light and engaged the whole time. That is flow at work.

Key Takeaways

- Flow is the state of optimal performance where focus, skill, and challenge align.
- Traders can increase the likelihood of entering flow by setting clear goals, reducing distractions, and trading within their skill level.
- Peak performance requires preparation, energy management, and recovery—not just skill.
- Flow is not luck—it is the result of intentional structure, discipline, and the right balance of challenge and capability.

15.3 Mindfulness & Emotional Mastery

In trading, most mistakes come not from a lack of knowledge, but from a lack of emotional control. Fear, greed, impatience, and overconfidence often lead traders to deviate from their strategies. To achieve long-term success, traders must learn the art of **emotional mastery**—the ability to remain calm, clear, and disciplined under pressure. One of the most effective paths to this mastery is through **mindfulness**.

What is Mindfulness in Trading?

Mindfulness is the practice of being fully aware and present in the moment without judgment. For traders, this means:

- Observing market movements without reacting impulsively.
- Recognizing emotions (fear, greed, frustration) as they arise, without letting them control decisions.
- Developing the space between stimulus (a price move, news headline) and response (a trading decision).

Instead of being swept away by emotional impulses, mindfulness allows traders to act with intention and alignment to their plan.

Why Emotional Mastery Matters in Trading

The markets are uncertain, and volatility naturally triggers emotional responses. Traders who lack emotional mastery often fall into predictable traps:

- **Fear:** Cutting winners too early or avoiding valid trades.
- **Greed:** Overleveraging, revenge trading, or ignoring risk rules.
- **Impatience:** Entering trades without proper setups.
- **Overconfidence:** Abandoning risk management after a series of wins.

Emotional mastery doesn't mean eliminating feelings—it means acknowledging them without letting them dictate behavior.

Practical Mindfulness Techniques for Traders

1. **Pre-Market Meditation:** Begin each trading session with 5–10 minutes of deep breathing to center your mind.
2. **Mindful Pauses:** Before executing a trade, pause for a breath. Ask: "Am I following my plan or reacting emotionally?"
3. **Emotion Journaling:** Record not only your trades, but also your emotional state during the trade. Over time, patterns of emotional triggers will emerge.
4. **Visualization:** Rehearse market scenarios mentally. Imagine how you will calmly execute your plan if the market spikes against you.
5. **Body Awareness:** Notice physical signals of stress—racing heartbeat, sweaty palms, muscle tension—and use breathing to reset.

Case Example: Practicing Emotional Discipline

Arjun, a trader, often exited trades too early whenever profits appeared, fearing reversal. Through mindfulness practice, he learned to notice the fear in real-time—tightness in his chest and anxious thoughts. Instead of reacting, he paused, took three deep breaths, and revisited his trade plan. With practice, he stopped letting fear dominate his decisions and allowed profitable trades to reach their targets.

From Mindfulness to Mastery

Mindfulness builds the foundation for emotional mastery, but mastery comes with consistent practice. Over time, traders develop:

- **Awareness:** Recognizing emotions as they arise.

- **Detachment:** Understanding that emotions are signals, not commands.
- **Control:** Acting based on strategy and probability, not emotion.

This level of mastery creates consistency, reduces stress, and enhances decision-making even in the most volatile conditions.

Key Takeaways

- Mindfulness is the practice of staying present and aware without judgment.
- Emotional mastery in trading is about recognizing emotions but not being ruled by them.
- Fear, greed, impatience, and overconfidence are the main emotional traps.
- Techniques such as meditation, journaling, and mindful pauses help traders stay calm and disciplined.
- True mastery develops with practice, leading to consistent, rational, and resilient decision-making.

Key Takeaways

- **Psychological strength is as critical as technical skill.** Advanced traders differentiate themselves not just by strategies, but by the ability to stay resilient, focused, and calm under pressure.
- **Mental conditioning builds resilience.** Through consistent practice, exposure to controlled stress, and reflective journaling, traders develop the toughness needed to withstand losses and keep executing their plan.
- **Flow state enables peak performance.** By combining preparation, focus, and structured routines, traders can reach a mental state where actions feel effortless, decisions are clear, and distractions fade away.
- **Mindfulness is the gateway to emotional mastery.** Rather than suppressing emotions, successful traders recognize them in real-time

and choose disciplined, data-driven actions instead of impulsive reactions.

- **Fear, greed, impatience, and overconfidence** are the four dominant psychological traps. Recognizing and managing them through mindfulness, visualization, and discipline is key to consistency.

- **Sustainable trading success requires inner balance.** Mental clarity, emotional control, and psychological resilience create the foundation for executing strategies with precision, even in volatile or uncertain conditions.

- Advanced psychology transforms trading from a stressful pursuit into a disciplined craft—allowing traders to operate with confidence, adaptability, and long-term consistency.

Chapter 16

Developing Your Trading Plan

Introduction

Learning strategies, managing risk, and understanding market psychology are all essential skills, but without a structured trading plan, even experienced traders can struggle with consistency. A trading plan serves as a personal roadmap, detailing entry and exit criteria, risk limits, position sizing, and daily routines. It transforms knowledge into actionable steps, helps control emotions, and ensures disciplined execution under varying market conditions. In this chapter, we will explore how to create a robust trading plan, tailor it to your goals, and integrate all the lessons you have learned so far into a practical, repeatable system.

A Story: Turning Knowledge into Action

Arjun had learned strategies, risk management, and psychology, but his trading was inconsistent. His mentor advised: "All knowledge is useless without a plan. A trading plan is your roadmap — it tells you what to do, when, and how." A well-crafted plan increases discipline, reduces emotional decisions, and improves long-term results.

16.1 Setting Realistic Goals

A trading plan is only as effective as the goals that guide it. Many beginner traders fail not because they lack strategies, but because they set unrealistic or vague objectives. Goals give direction, help maintain discipline, and provide a way to measure progress over time. Without them, even well-executed trades can feel aimless, and emotions often take over.

The Importance of Realistic Goals

Realistic goals are crucial because trading involves uncertainty, volatility, and the possibility of losses. Overly ambitious targets often lead to excessive risk-taking, overtrading, or frustration. Conversely, goals that are too modest can result in complacency or slow growth. Striking the right balance ensures sustainable learning and performance improvement.

SMART Goals Framework

Effective trading goals should follow the SMART framework:

- **Specific:** Clearly define what you want to achieve. For example, instead of "Make money trading," say "Grow my trading account by 5% each month."
- **Measurable:** Ensure progress can be tracked with quantifiable metrics, such as account balance, number of successful trades, or risk-adjusted returns.
- **Achievable:** Set targets that are challenging but attainable given your capital, experience, and market conditions.
- **Relevant:** Goals should align with your overall financial objectives, lifestyle, and risk tolerance.
- **Time-bound:** Assign a clear timeframe to your goals, which encourages discipline and focus.

Types of Trading Goals

Financial Goals: These focus on profit, account growth, or risk-adjusted returns. Example: "Increase my trading account from $10,000 to $12,000 in 6 months while keeping maximum drawdown below 5%."

Skill-Based Goals: These focus on improving your trading ability. Example: "Consistently identify at least three high-probability setups per week and execute them according to my plan."

Behavioral Goals: These target emotional control, discipline, and habit formation. Example: "Keep a detailed trading journal for 90 consecutive days and review it weekly for mistakes and improvements."

Balancing Ambition and Realism

It is natural to want rapid profits, but the market does not reward impatience. Overestimating your abilities or expecting extraordinary returns can lead to unnecessary risk-taking. For example, attempting a 20% monthly return with $10,000 may tempt you to use high leverage and aggressive trades. A more sustainable approach might be targeting 2–5% monthly, allowing room for mistakes, learning, and controlled risk exposure.

Example of Realistic Goal Setting

Suppose you are a new trader with a $10,000 account. You decide to:

1. Allocate 2% risk per trade (i.e., $200 maximum loss per trade).
2. Aim for an average monthly return of 3–4%.
3. Focus on mastering swing trading strategies and chart patterns for the next 6 months.
4. Maintain a trading journal and review all trades weekly.

This plan balances financial ambition with learning objectives and risk control, providing a clear roadmap for progress.

Key Takeaways

- Realistic goals guide your trading decisions and improve discipline.
- Use the SMART framework to define financial, skill-based, and behavioral objectives.
- Balance ambition with practicality to avoid frustration and reckless risk-taking.
- Document your goals and track progress to ensure accountability and continuous improvement.

16.2 Trading Rules and Checklist

Successful trading is not just about finding the right setups or using advanced indicators — it's about following consistent rules and having a disciplined approach. Trading rules act as guardrails, ensuring that emotions, biases, or impulsive decisions do not derail your strategy. A checklist complements these rules by providing a step-by-step guide to evaluate every trade before execution.

Why Trading Rules Matter

Trading rules define what you will and will not do in the market. They help:

- Maintain discipline during volatile market conditions.
- Avoid overtrading or revenge trading after losses.
- Protect capital by enforcing risk management principles.
- Establish a repeatable process that can be refined over time.

Core Trading Rules

1. **Risk Management:** Never risk more than your predetermined percentage per trade (e.g., 1–2% of your capital).
2. **Trade Setup Confirmation:** Enter trades only when your criteria, such as technical patterns, indicators, or fundamental triggers, are met.
3. **Position Sizing:** Calculate position size according to risk per trade and stop-loss levels.
4. **Avoid Emotional Trades:** Never enter a trade out of fear, greed, or revenge.
5. **Adhere to Stop-Loss and Take-Profit Levels:** Protect your capital and lock in profits automatically without second-guessing.
6. **Keep a Trading Journal:** Document the rationale, execution, and outcome of every trade. This is critical for learning and improvement.

Creating a Pre-Trade Checklist

A pre-trade checklist ensures every trade is evaluated objectively. Example items to include:

- Market conditions favorable (trend, volatility, liquidity)?
- Trade setup confirmed by indicators or patterns?
- Risk/reward ratio acceptable (e.g., at least 1:2)?
- Stop-loss and take-profit levels defined?
- Position size calculated according to risk tolerance?
- No significant news or events that could affect the trade unexpectedly?
- Emotional state: calm, focused, and disciplined?

Example of a Checklist in Action

Suppose you identify a bullish breakout on a stock chart:

1. Check trend and volatility: Confirm upward momentum.
2. Confirm setup: Price broke resistance with volume spike.
3. Calculate position: Risking 2% of $10,000 = $200.
4. Set stop-loss: Below the breakout level.
5. Define take-profit: At the next resistance zone for a 1:2 risk/reward ratio.
6. Review market news: No earnings or announcements expected today.
7. Evaluate emotions: Calm and focused.
8. Execute trade only if all checklist items are satisfied.

Key Takeaways

- Consistent trading rules and checklists reduce mistakes and emotional decision-making.
- Pre-trade evaluation ensures every trade is aligned with your strategy and risk tolerance.
- Maintaining discipline and following a structured process is often more important than predicting market direction.

16.3 Journaling and Tracking Performance

Consistently profitable trading is not about luck — it is about learning from every decision, trade, and outcome. A well-maintained trading journal allows you to track performance, identify patterns, and improve decision-making over time. Think of it as the "logbook" of your trading journey.

Why Journaling Matters

- **Accountability:** Documenting every trade forces you to take responsibility for your decisions.
- **Pattern Recognition:** Tracking results helps reveal strengths, weaknesses, and recurring mistakes.
- **Emotional Awareness:** Recording your emotional state during trades helps identify how feelings influence decisions.
- **Strategy Refinement:** Journals allow testing and improving trading strategies over time.

What to Include in a Trading Journal

- **Trade Details:** Asset, entry and exit price, position size, stop-loss, take-profit levels.
- **Rationale:** Why you entered the trade — technical setup, fundamental reason, news event.
- **Market Conditions:** Trend, volatility, news, and time of day.
- **Emotional State:** Calm, anxious, greedy, fearful — any emotion affecting your decision.
- **Outcome:** Profit/loss, what went well, what could be improved.
- **Notes:** Lessons learned or adjustments for future trades.

Sample Journal Entry

- **Asset:** Tesla (TSLA)
- **Entry Price:** $720

- **Exit Price:** \$735
- **Position Size:** 10 shares
- **Stop-Loss:** \$710
- **Take-Profit:** \$735
- **Rationale:** Breakout above resistance with high volume
- **Market Conditions:** Bullish trend, moderate volatility
- **Emotional State:** Confident and calm
- **Outcome:** Profit \$150, trade executed according to plan
- **Notes:** Good adherence to rules; consider tighter stop in volatile markets

Tips for Effective Journaling

- Be consistent: Journal every trade, even small ones.
- Include both successes and failures: Lessons come from both.
- Use digital tools if possible: Excel, TradingView, or dedicated journaling apps.
- Review weekly: Identify patterns and adjust your strategy accordingly.

Key Takeaways

- Journaling transforms experience into actionable insights and improves discipline.
- Tracking performance helps quantify strengths, weaknesses, and the effectiveness of strategies.
- Regular reflection ensures continuous learning and long-term trading growth.

16.4 Continuous Learning: Books, Courses, Mentors

Trading is a journey, not a destination. Markets evolve, strategies shift, and new tools emerge. To stay ahead, continuous learning is essential. Knowledge compounds like capital — the more you invest in it, the greater your long-term edge.

1. Books

- **Purpose:** Provide foundational knowledge, strategies, and insights from experienced traders and investors.
- **Recommended Approach:** Read a mix of theory (e.g., technical analysis, risk management) and case studies (real trades, market history).
- **Example:** Studying "Technical Analysis of the Financial Markets" by John Murphy helps understand chart patterns and indicator interpretation.

2. Courses

- **Purpose:** Structured, interactive learning with practical exercises, simulations, and mentor guidance.
- **Types:**
  - Online courses (Udemy, Coursera, or Trading Academy programs)
  - Workshops or webinars with live market examples
  - Specialized courses in options, futures, or algorithmic trading
- **Example:** A course on "Algorithmic Trading in Python" teaches how to backtest strategies and automate trades.

3. Mentors

- **Purpose:** Accelerate learning by gaining insights, feedback, and accountability from experienced traders.
- **Benefits:** Mentors provide guidance on strategy selection, risk management, and psychological challenges.

- **Example:** Weekly calls with a mentor reviewing your journal can highlight blind spots, emotional biases, and improvement opportunities.

4. Self-Directed Learning and Practice

- Combine reading, courses, and mentorship with hands-on practice using demo accounts and simulations.
- Experimentation allows testing strategies without risking real capital, turning theory into experience.
- Track progress and update your trading plan based on lessons learned.

Key Takeaways

- Continuous learning is essential for adapting to changing markets and improving performance.
- Books, courses, and mentors each serve unique roles — combining them maximizes your knowledge and skill development.
- Practical application through journaling, simulations, and real trades solidifies learning.

Exercise: Draft a Personal 30-Day Trading Plan

Creating a structured trading plan transforms knowledge into consistent action. This exercise guides you to draft a 30-day plan tailored to your goals, risk tolerance, and preferred strategies.

Step 1: Define Your Goals

- Specify measurable objectives for the next 30 days (e.g., "Execute 10 demo trades with proper risk management" or "Identify three repeatable setups in Forex").
- Decide if your focus is on learning, consistency, or profit.

Step 2: Choose Markets and Instruments

- Pick 1–3 markets or instruments you will trade (e.g., EUR/USD, Bitcoin, or Apple stock).

- Keep it simple initially to avoid spreading your focus too thin.

Step 3: Define Entry and Exit Criteria

- Identify your preferred strategies (trend following, swing trading, breakout, etc.).
- Set rules for entries, stop losses, and take profits.
- Include conditions for skipping trades if the setup is unclear.

Step 4: Risk Management

- Define your risk per trade (1–2% rule) and maximum daily loss.
- Specify position sizing rules and portfolio exposure limits.

Step 5: Journaling and Review

- Commit to logging every trade with:
  - Entry and exit prices
  - Trade rationale
  - Outcome and emotions
- Schedule weekly reviews to identify patterns, mistakes, and improvements.

Step 6: Learning and Adjustment

- After 30 days, analyze performance and adjust your plan based on lessons learned.
- Repeat the cycle, gradually refining your strategies and discipline.

Key Takeaways

- A detailed trading plan increases discipline, reduces emotional decisions, and improves long-term results.
- Even small, structured steps over 30 days compound into meaningful learning and skill development.
- Regular review and adjustment ensure your plan evolves with your experience and market conditions.

Key Takeaways

- A well-crafted trading plan is essential to transform knowledge into consistent action.
- Setting clear, measurable goals keeps your focus on learning and disciplined execution rather than chasing profits.
- Defining markets, instruments, and strategies limits confusion and allows for deeper understanding.
- Risk management rules, including position sizing and stop-loss limits, protect capital and reduce emotional decision-making.
- Journaling every trade with rationale, outcome, and emotional state provides critical feedback for improvement.
- Regular review and adjustment of your plan help refine strategies and adapt to changing market conditions.
- Even short, 30-day structured plans create compounding learning effects and build long-term trading competence.

Part VI

Real-World Trading Case Studies

Chapter 17

Real-world Trade Examples

Introduction

Theory builds the foundation, but trading mastery comes from seeing how concepts play out in actual markets. Charts, strategies, and risk management rules mean little until they are applied in real-world situations where emotions, uncertainty, and execution challenges exist.

In this chapter, we move from abstract knowledge to practical application. By walking through detailed trade examples across stocks, forex, and crypto, you will see how traders analyze setups, make decisions, manage risk, and learn from both wins and losses. The goal is not to copy these trades, but to train your eye to spot opportunities and develop your own judgment as a trader.

A Story: Learning from Real Trades

Rohan, a new trader, often studied theory but struggled to connect it with real market behavior. By analyzing real trades, including successes and failures, he began to understand patterns, risk, and the importance of execution.

17.1 Stock Trades: Entry, Exit, Lessons

Practical skill in stock trading comes from studying many real trades — winners, losers, and the messy middle. Below are richly detailed, multi-scenario examples that show how traders identify setups, size positions, place stops and targets, manage the trade, and extract lessons afterward. Each example includes concrete numbers (assuming a $10,000 trading account unless otherwise stated), position-sizing using the 1–2% rule, and a short post-trade checklist.

Example 1 — Momentum Breakout (Trend & Volume Confirmation)

Setup & Rationale: Stock: **AAPL**. Price has consolidated between $360–$370 for two weeks. Volume contracts during consolidation, then a strong green daily candle closes at $372 on above-average volume — classic breakout.

Plan:

- Entry: $372 (close above resistance).
- Stop-loss: $355 (below consolidation) — $17 risk per share.
- Risk per trade: 1% of $10,000 = $100.
- Position size: $100 / $17 = 5.88 ⇒ **5 shares** (round down).
- Initial target: measured move = consolidation height ($370-$360= $10) projected → $382; secondary target $400.
- Execution rule: take 50% off at first target, trail stop on remainder.

Outcome (illustrative): Price hits $382 (partial profit booked), then continues to $420 over weeks; trailing stop locks remaining profit; final P&L: +$235 (after partial take and trailing).

Lessons:

- Volume confirmation reduces false-breakout risk.
- Position sizing based on dollar-risk keeps the loss limited if breakout fails.
- Partial-profit-taking balances locking gains and letting winners run.

Example 2 — Swing Trade on Pullback (Support, RSI Confirmation)

Setup & Rationale: Stock: **TSLA**. Long-term uptrend; price pulls back near a rising trendline and the 21-day EMA. RSI dips to 32 (near oversold for the trend).

Plan:

- Entry: \$750 on candle showing rejection of support.
- Stop-loss: \$720 (below trendline) — \$30 risk per share.
- Risk per trade: 1% = \$100.
- Position size: \$100 / \$30 = 3.33 ⇒ **3 shares**.
- Target: resistance at \$820 (risk–reward ≈ 2.3:1).
- Management: move stop to breakeven after 50% of target achieved; trail thereafter.

Outcome (illustrative): Trade reaches target after 12 days. Net profit ≈ (820-750)*3 = \$210, after fees.

Lessons:

- In trending markets, buying pullbacks with confirmation (price action + RSI) increases success probability.
- Small position sizes due to wider stop avoid overexposure.

Example 3 — Earnings Play (Event Risk & Hedging)

Setup & Rationale: Stock: **Company B**. Earnings due on Friday. Consensus shows high volatility potential.

Two approaches:

1. **Conservative:** Stay flat (no position) to avoid binary risk.
2. **Speculative with Hedge:** Buy shares and buy protective puts (insurance).

Hedged Plan (if speculative):

- Buy 10 shares at \$220 (position value \$2,200).

- Buy 1 put with \$210 strike expiring shortly for premium \$40 (cost = \$40).
- Effective worst-case loss = premium + difference to strike if stock collapses.
- Hedging cost reduces upside but caps downside; risk management must account for premium in P&L.

Outcome (illustrative): Earnings miss → stock gaps to \$185. Without hedge: loss per share = \$35; with put, the put gains offset most loss, net loss limited to premium + small gap slippage.

Lessons:

- Earnings are binary events — hedges control tail risk.
- Never ignore the cost of hedging in expectancy calculations.
- For small accounts, option minimums and costs may make hedging impractical.

Example 4 — Gap-Up Fade (Intraday Risk & Execution)

Setup & Rationale: Stock: **Company C**. Opens +8% on news. Many retail traders chase intraday; institutional selling often causes a fade.

Plan:

- Avoid chasing the immediate open. Wait 20–60 minutes for price behavior (volume, VWAP).
- If price fails to hold above VWAP and shows lower highs, consider short with tight stop.
- Example: Entry short at \$310, stop at \$316 (six-dollar risk), target \$295.
- Position sizing: with wide intraday volatility, risk per trade = 0.5–1% recommended.

Outcome (illustrative): Stock fades to \$292 intraday → profit captured. However, chasing at open could have led to slippage and spread costs.

Lessons:

- Chasing gap-ups increases slippage and execution risk; wait for confirmation.
- Intraday trades need tighter stops and smaller position sizes.

Example 5 — Mean Reversion (Oversold Bounce)

Setup & Rationale: Stock: **Mid-cap retailer**. Rapid 12% sell-off over two days. Price hits lower Bollinger Band and RSI 20. Look for a mean-reversion bounce in a non-broken long-term trend.

Plan:

- Entry: on reversal candle + volume increase at \$48.
- Stop-loss: \$45 (below recent low) — \$3 risk.
- Risk per trade: 1% = \$100 $\rightarrow$ shares = 100/3 = 33 shares.
- Target: mean (20-day MA) at \$55 (RR 2.3:1).

Outcome: Bounce to \$55 over 10 days; trade profitable.

Lessons:

- Mean reversion works best when the longer-term trend is intact.
- Confirm reversal with volume and price structure, not only indicator extremes.

Example 6 — Trend-Following with Moving-Average Crossover

Setup & Rationale: Stock: **Industrial ETF**. 50-day EMA crosses above 200-day EMA (golden cross) on rising volume.

Plan:

- Entry: on confirmation day close above both EMAs at \$40.
- Stop-loss: 200-day EMA or 8% below entry, whichever is tighter.
- Risk per trade: 2% allowed for trend trades = \$200 risk.
- Use larger position size if volatility allows (e.g., risk per share = \$3 $\rightarrow$ 66 shares).
- Management: use wide trailing stop (e.g., 50-day low) to stay in the trend.

Outcome & Lessons:

- Trend trades may have lower win rate but larger winners—use wider stops and smaller number of positions.

- Be patient: trend following requires tolerance for drawdowns and patience while letting winners run.

Example 7 — Long-Term Value / Buy-and-Hold

Setup & Rationale: Stock: **Company D**. Strong fundamentals, discounted valuation after temporary headwind.

Plan:

- Allocate 5–10% of portfolio (long-term allocation), not governed by 1% intraday rule.
- Entry at $120; plan to hold 1–3 years unless fundamentals deteriorate.
- Use dollar-cost averaging to reduce timing risk.

Outcome & Lessons:

- Value investing requires conviction and larger tolerance for temporary volatility.
- Position sizing is driven by allocation strategy, not per-trade stop-risk calculus.

Example 8 — Pairs Trade (Market-Neutral Stock Pair)

Setup & Rationale: Stocks: **Retailer A (long)** vs **Retailer B (short)**. Historically correlated; current spread is wider than usual.

Plan:

- Go long the underperformer and short the outperformer to profit from spread mean reversion.
- Size positions to be dollar- and beta-neutral (calculate sensitivities).
- Example sizing: if Retailer A beta = 1.0 and Retailer B beta = 0.9, size short slightly smaller to neutralize market exposure.
- Stop based on spread widening beyond a threshold; target when spread reverts to historical mean.

Outcome & Lessons:

- Pairs trading manages market risk but introduces relative-risk; requires rigorous correlation and risk monitoring.

- Unexpected structural breaks (industry shock) can make correlations fail.

Standard Trade Journal Template (one-line per trade)

Date	Ticker	Strategy	Entry	Stop	Size	Exit	P&L
2025-09-01	AAPL	Breakout	372	355	5 sh	420	+$235
2025-09-10	TSLA	Pullback	750	720	3 sh	820	+$210

Pre-Trade Checklist (use before every stock trade)

1. Does the trade fit one of my documented strategies? (trend, breakout, mean-reversion, event-driven, value)
2. Is the market condition supportive (trend, volatility, liquidity)?
3. Entry, Stop, and Target defined? Is R:R acceptable (prefer $\geq$ 2:1)?
4. Position size computed using risk per trade rule (e.g., 1%) and stop distance?
5. Any scheduled news or earnings that increase risk?
6. Am I emotionally neutral and following the plan?

Post-Trade Review Questions

- Was the trade executed according to the plan? If not, why?
- Did I follow my stop-loss and position-size rules?
- What worked and what didn't in the setup or execution?
- What can I change to improve the next similar trade?

Key Takeaways

- **Plan before you act:** Define entry, stop, target, position size, and management rules ahead of execution.
- **Size by risk, not by capital:** Use the dollar-risk approach (1–2% rule) to compute shares/lot size.

- **Match strategy to market:** Trend-following, mean-reversion, event-driven, and value approaches work in different conditions — pick the right tool for the environment.
- **Use confirmation for higher-probability entries:** volume, momentum, and price-action confirmation reduce false signals.
- **Journal and review:** Every trade is a data point — analyze it objectively to improve your edge.
- **Manage expectations:** Not every trade will win; focus on expectancy (win rate $\times$ avg win $\times$ loss rate $\times$ avg loss) and consistent application of rules.

17.2 Forex Trades: Risk & Leverage

The foreign exchange (Forex) market is one of the most liquid markets in the world, trading over \$6 trillion daily. It offers unique opportunities for traders, but also introduces amplified risks due to leverage, volatility, and macroeconomic drivers. In this section, we explore how risk and leverage work in Forex, and illustrate them with practical examples.

Understanding Leverage in Forex

Unlike stock trading where leverage is typically 2:1, Forex brokers often offer leverage as high as 50:1, 100:1, or even 500:1. This means that with just \$1,000 of capital, a trader can control positions worth \$50,000 to \$500,000.

Example:

- Account equity = \$5,000.
- Broker leverage = 100:1.
- Maximum position size = \$5,000 $\times$ 100 = \$500,000 (but this is highly dangerous).

While this makes Forex appealing, it magnifies both profits and losses. A 1% adverse move in a \$100,000 position equals \$1,000, which is 20% of a \$5,000 account — potentially wiping out the trader in just a few trades.

Position Sizing Formula in Forex

The foundation of risk management is knowing *lot size*. A standard Forex lot = 100,000 units of base currency. Mini lot = 10,000 units. Micro lot = 1,000 units.

$$PositionSize(lots) = \frac{AccountRisk(\$)}{Stop - loss(pips) \times PipValue(\$/pip)}$$

Example:

- Account: \$10,000. Risk per trade: 1% = \$100.
- Stop-loss: 50 pips.
- Pip value (EUR/USD, mini lot): \$1 per pip.
- Position size = \$100 / (50 × 1) = 2 mini lots = 20,000 units.

This keeps the maximum loss capped at \$100, regardless of leverage.

Trade Example 1 — EUR/USD Trend Trade

Setup: EUR/USD is trending up. Trader identifies breakout above resistance at 1.0850.

Plan:

- Entry: 1.0850.
- Stop-loss: 1.0800 (50 pips).
- Target: 1.0950 (100 pips).
- Account: \$5,000. Risk 1% = \$50.
- Pip value = \$1 (per mini lot).
- Position size = 1 mini lot (50 pip risk = \$50).

Outcome: Price rallies to 1.0950 → +100 pips = +\$100. Risk–reward = 1:2. Consistent with good trading practice.

Lesson: Position sizing keeps the loss manageable. Even with 100:1 leverage available, disciplined use prevents wipeouts.

Trade Example 2 — GBP/USD Overleveraged Loss

Setup: Trader with \$2,000 account risks too much on GBP/USD, using 1 standard lot (100,000 units).

Plan:

- Entry: 1.2500.
- Stop-loss: 1.2450 (50 pips).
- Pip value = \$10 (per standard lot).
- Loss if stopped = 50 pips × \$10 = \$500.

Outcome: Stop triggered → loss = \$500 (25% of account). After 4 such losses, account is nearly wiped out.

Lesson: Using maximum leverage is financial suicide. Small accounts must avoid standard lots.

Trade Example 3 — USD/JPY Event Trade with Controlled Risk

Setup: U.S. Non-Farm Payrolls (NFP) released. High volatility expected.

Plan:

- Account: \$10,000. Risk = 1% = \$100.
- Entry: Buy USD/JPY at 145.00.
- Stop-loss: 144.50 (50 pips).
- Pip value = \$1 (mini lot).
- Position size = 2 mini lots (risk = \$100).

Outcome: Price surges to 146.50 → +150 pips = +\$300. Risk–reward = 1:3.

Lesson: Event trades can be profitable if risk is capped and not oversized.

Common Forex Risk Management Rules

- Never risk more than 1–2% of account per trade.
- Use stop-loss orders religiously — Forex is 24/5 and moves fast.
- Treat leverage as optional — not as a weapon to maximize profits.

- Avoid holding large leveraged positions overnight due to rollover fees and gaps.
- Track exposure across correlated pairs (EUR/USD, GBP/USD, AUD/USD). Multiple trades can compound risk.

Key Takeaways

- Leverage is a double-edged sword — it magnifies both profits and losses.
- Position sizing formulas prevent catastrophic losses.
- Pip values, stop-loss distance, and account risk determine lot size — not "gut feeling."
- Overleveraging is the single most common reason retail traders blow up their Forex accounts.
- Controlled leverage with strict risk management is the key to longevity in Forex.

17.3 Crypto Trades: Volatility & Timing

Cryptocurrency markets are unique due to extreme volatility and 24/7 trading. This creates high profit potential but also significant risk, making timing, strategy, and risk management critical.

Market Characteristics

- **24/7 Trading:** Continuous operation requires awareness of positions at all times.
- **High Volatility:** Prices can move 5–10% or more within a day.
- **Liquidity Variance:** Popular coins like BTC/ETH are highly liquid; smaller altcoins may experience slippage.
- **News Sensitivity:** Regulatory updates, exchange outages, or social media can trigger rapid movements.

Trading Strategies

- **Trend Following:** Trade in the direction of momentum using moving averages, MACD, or RSI.
- **Breakout Trading:** Enter when price breaks key support/resistance levels.
- **Swing Trading:** Capture short- to medium-term price swings within a trend.
- **Scalping:** Quick trades to profit from minor intraday fluctuations.

Risk Management

- Always use stop-loss orders to limit losses.
- Avoid excessive leverage; derivatives can amplify both gains and losses.
- Use smaller position sizes due to higher volatility.

Example Trades

Trade 1: Bitcoin Breakout Riya notices BTC breaking above $35,000:

- Buys 0.5 BTC at $35,100
- Stop-loss at $34,000
- Profit target at $38,000

Outcome: Price hits $38,000, earning a controlled profit with limited risk.

Trade 2: Ethereum Swing Trade Arjun sees ETH bouncing off a support level around $2,500:

- Buys 2 ETH at $2,510
- Stop-loss at $2,450
- Targets $2,700

Outcome: ETH reaches $2,700 over two days; trade captures a 7.6% gain.

Trade 3: Altcoin Scalping Neha identifies a low-cap coin showing intraday volatility:

- Buys 1,000 units at $0.80

- Sets tight stop-loss at $0.78
- Sells at $0.85 after a 3-hour spike

Outcome: Quick 6.25% profit, demonstrating scalping potential in volatile altcoins.

Lessons Learned

- Volatility can be an advantage if risk is controlled.
- Multiple strategies can coexist: breakout, swing, and scalping.
- Proper stop-loss placement and position sizing are essential to protect capital.
- 24/7 monitoring and adaptability are required for crypto markets.

Exercise: Analyze Screenshots of Past Trades

One of the most effective ways to build trading intuition is by reviewing past trades — both winning and losing. Screenshots (or chart captures) of trades provide a visual record of how setups looked in real time, how entries and exits were chosen, and what went right or wrong.

Instructions

1. Select at least 5 past trades from your demo or live account.
2. For each trade, capture the chart at the moment of entry, including indicators, support/resistance levels, and candlestick structure.
3. Record key details in your journal:
    - Date and instrument traded.
    - Entry price, stop-loss, and take-profit levels.
    - Position size and risk per trade.
    - Outcome in pips/$ and percentage of account.
4. Annotate the screenshot with notes on why you took the trade.
5. After the trade is closed, review the chart again:

- Did the setup follow your plan?
- Was your stop-loss and take-profit placement logical?
- Did emotions (fear, greed, hesitation) play a role?
- What would you do differently next time?

Goal

By analyzing screenshots, you will:

- Recognize repeating chart patterns and setups.
- Identify emotional or impulsive mistakes visually.
- Build a personalized "playbook" of strategies that work best for you.

Pro Tip

Create a digital folder labeled by strategy (e.g., "Breakouts," "Trend Trades," "False Signals"). Over time, this becomes a personal database of lessons — your own trading encyclopedia.

Key Takeaways

- Real-world trade reviews bridge the gap between theory and practice.
- Studying both **winning and losing trades** is essential to refine strategies.
- Screenshots and journals provide a **visual and written record** that help identify repeating setups and mistakes.
- Consistent review builds a personal **trading playbook** — a collection of lessons unique to your style.
- The goal is not just to find what works, but also to eliminate what doesn't, saving time and capital in the long run.

Chapter 18

Common Mistakes & How to Avoid Them

Introduction

Every trader, whether beginner or experienced, faces setbacks. The difference between success and failure often lies not in avoiding mistakes altogether, but in recognizing them early and learning from them. This chapter highlights the most frequent errors traders make—from letting emotions dictate decisions to ignoring risk management—and provides practical strategies to sidestep them. By internalizing these lessons, you can shorten your learning curve, protect your capital, and trade with greater confidence.

A Story: Learning from Mistakes

Sameer was enthusiastic about trading but quickly realized that mistakes were costing him more than missed opportunities. He compiled a list of common pitfalls, reflecting on each trade and the emotional triggers behind them. Learning to avoid these mistakes dramatically improved his results.

18.1 Emotional Trading

Emotions are one of the greatest challenges traders face. While strategies and tools can be learned, controlling fear, greed, and impulses requires discipline and self-awareness. Emotional trading is often the hidden reason behind losses, even when the analysis was correct. Below we break down the key emotional traps, real-world scenarios, and methods to overcome them.

1. Fear of Missing Out (FOMO)

Definition: The urge to enter a trade because others appear to be profiting, without proper analysis. **Example:** A trader sees a stock rapidly rising and buys in late at the top, only to face a sudden reversal. **How to Avoid:**

- Remind yourself that opportunities are endless; missing one trade is not the end.
- Stick to pre-set rules for entries; avoid impulsive market chasing.
- Analyze risk–reward before every entry, even under time pressure.

2. Revenge Trading

Definition: Entering trades after a loss to "win back" money quickly, often without logic. **Example:** After losing INR 10,000 in the morning, a trader doubles position size in the afternoon, hoping to recover, but ends up compounding losses. **How to Avoid:**

- Accept losses as part of trading — not as something to "recover" immediately.
- Set a daily stop-loss limit (e.g., max 2% of capital); stop trading once reached.
- Pause after a loss; review what went wrong before considering the next move.

3. Overconfidence

Definition: After a streak of wins, traders believe every trade will succeed and ignore risk controls. **Example:** A forex trader makes three profitable trades in a row and then risks 20% of capital on the next trade — which fails. **How to Avoid:**

- Stick to consistent position sizing regardless of past wins.
- Regularly remind yourself that probabilities, not certainty, govern markets.
- Maintain humility — no one wins all the time.

4. Fear of Loss

Definition: Closing trades too early or hesitating to take valid setups due to fear of losing money. **Example:** A trader sets a stop-loss but exits the trade prematurely for a small profit, only to see the market hit their original target. **How to Avoid:**

- Trust your analysis; avoid second-guessing once the trade is live.
- Use trailing stops to secure profits while letting trades run.
- Build confidence by backtesting and paper trading strategies.

5. Greed and Holding Too Long

Definition: Staying in profitable trades longer than planned in hopes of higher gains, often leading to reversals. **Example:** A trader has a target of 10% but refuses to exit when it's hit, holding out for 15%. The price reverses and turns profit into loss. **How to Avoid:**

- Define targets before entering and exit at pre-decided levels.
- Partial profit booking — sell some at the target, let the rest run with a stop.
- Train yourself to be satisfied with consistency, not jackpot trades.

6. Stress and Fatigue

Definition: Making decisions under exhaustion or stress, reducing objectivity and patience. **Example:** A trader spends 12 hours staring at screens, makes careless entries late at night, and suffers repeated losses. **How to Avoid:**

- Trade during your most alert hours; avoid overtrading.
- Set clear daily trading hours; do not chase markets 24/7.
- Balance trading with rest, exercise, and non-market activities.

Practical Tools to Manage Emotions

- **Trading Journal:** Record trades, reasons, and emotions felt — identify patterns over time.

- **Pre-Trade Checklist:** Confirm entry criteria, stop-loss, and target before execution.
- **Mindfulness & Breaks:** Short breaks, breathing exercises, or meditation to calm nerves.
- **Automation:** Use stop-loss and limit orders to remove emotional interference.

Summary: Emotional trading is not eliminated — it is managed. Traders who recognize triggers and implement discipline tools gain consistency. The goal is not to suppress emotions, but to prevent them from hijacking your trading decisions.

18.2 Overtrading

Overtrading occurs when a trader takes too many trades in a short period or risks excessive capital on each trade. It is a common pitfall, especially for beginners, and often stems from emotional impulses, boredom, or the desire to recover losses. Overtrading can quickly erode capital, increase transaction costs, and reduce decision quality.

1. Causes of Overtrading

- **Revenge Trading:** Attempting to recover losses with multiple impulsive trades.
- **Boredom:** Entering trades without proper setups because the trader feels idle.
- **Greed:** Chasing profits beyond the strategy's recommended frequency.
- **Lack of Plan:** Trading without a pre-defined strategy or checklist.

2. Signs You Are Overtrading

- Entering trades without analysis or skipping the checklist.
- Increasing trade size beyond normal risk limits.
- Constantly watching screens and making reactive decisions.
- Emotional volatility after every trade, including minor losses.

3. Risks and Consequences

- **Capital Erosion:** Frequent small losses can accumulate faster than occasional big losses.
- **Increased Costs:** Higher commissions, spreads, and slippage reduce net profits.
- **Decision Fatigue:** Cognitive overload can impair judgment, leading to poor trades.
- **Strategy Breakdown:** The effectiveness of well-tested strategies decreases under overtrading.

4. How to Prevent Overtrading

- **Follow a Trading Plan:** Only trade setups that meet your defined criteria.
- **Set Trade Limits:** Define maximum trades per day/week and stick to them.
- **Risk Management:** Adhere to position sizing and stop-loss rules.
- **Scheduled Breaks:** Avoid long hours staring at screens; take periodic mental breaks.
- **Review and Reflect:** Keep a trading journal to identify patterns of overtrading.

5. Example Scenario

A trader has a rule to enter only trades with at least a 2:1 risk–reward ratio. After a small loss, they ignore the rule and take multiple trades with 1:1 risk–reward just to "make back" the loss. By the end of the day, they have 5 small losing trades and pay higher commissions, eroding their initial capital. This illustrates how overtrading can turn a disciplined strategy into a losing day.

6. Key Takeaways

- Overtrading is often emotional, not strategic.
- Discipline, pre-defined setups, and risk limits are the best defenses.

- Track your trades and recognize triggers that lead to overtrading.
- Quality always beats quantity in trading; one well-planned trade is better than several impulsive ones.

18.3 Ignoring Risk Management

Risk management is the backbone of sustainable trading. Ignoring it is one of the most common mistakes that leads to severe losses or even account wipeouts. Successful traders prioritize protecting capital over chasing profits.

1. Why Risk Management Matters

- **Preserves Capital:** Protecting your account ensures you can stay in the game long enough to profit.
- **Reduces Emotional Stress:** Knowing that losses are limited prevents panic decisions.
- **Maintains Strategy Effectiveness:** Even the best strategies fail without proper risk controls.
- **Enables Compound Growth:** Consistent risk management allows gradual account growth over time.

2. Common Risk Management Mistakes

- **No Stop-Losses:** Failing to define maximum loss per trade.
- **Over-Leveraging:** Taking positions too large relative to account size.
- **Ignoring Risk–Reward Ratio:** Entering trades where potential loss outweighs potential gain.
- **Concentrated Positions:** Investing too heavily in one trade or asset without diversification.

3. Principles of Effective Risk Management

- **Position Sizing:** Limit risk per trade (commonly 1–2% of capital).
- **Stop-Loss Orders:** Predefine exit points to control losses.

- **Risk–Reward Ratio:** Aim for trades where potential reward exceeds risk, ideally 2:1 or higher.
- **Diversification:** Spread exposure across different assets, sectors, or instruments.
- **Regular Review:** Continuously assess risk management effectiveness and adjust as needed.

4. Example Scenario

A trader ignores position sizing and risks 20% of their account on a single trade. The market moves against them, and the loss is substantial enough to require an aggressive recovery strategy. In contrast, if they had risked only 2% per trade, they could have survived the loss and continued trading without emotional distress.

5. Tips to Avoid Ignoring Risk Management

- Always define maximum acceptable loss before entering any trade.
- Use automated stop-loss and take-profit orders to enforce discipline.
- Review daily and weekly trades to ensure adherence to risk rules.
- Treat risk management as important as identifying trading opportunities.

6. Key Takeaways

- Protecting capital is more important than chasing profits.
- Ignoring risk management is a fast track to account destruction.
- Consistent use of stop-loss, proper position sizing, and risk–reward evaluation ensures long-term trading survival.
- Discipline and preparation differentiate professional traders from amateurs.

Case Study: 5 Traders, 5 Mistakes

Learning from real-life experiences is one of the fastest ways to internalize trading lessons. Below, we explore five traders, each making a common yet costly mistake. For each, we analyze what went wrong, why it happened, and how it could have been avoided.

1. **Trader 1: Overtrading**
   Ravi, a beginner, believed that more trades meant more opportunities to profit. He placed multiple trades daily without proper analysis, often entering impulsively. Transaction fees piled up, and he suffered losses from poorly timed trades.
   Analysis: Overtrading increases costs and exposes traders to unnecessary risk. Momentum and setups should guide trade frequency, not impulse.
   Takeaway: Stick to your strategy, limit trades to high-probability setups, and avoid trading out of boredom or emotion.

2. **Trader 2: Ignoring Risk Management**
   Priya had a winning strategy but ignored position sizing and stop-losses. A sudden market swing wiped out 30% of her capital in one trade.
   Analysis: Even a profitable strategy can fail if losses are unmanaged. Risk per trade should align with account size.
   Takeaway: Never risk more than a small percentage of your account per trade (1–2%). Use stop-losses and define risk-reward before entering.

3. **Trader 3: Emotional Trading**
   Akash followed a systematic trading plan but let greed and fear dictate his actions. After a winning streak, he increased position sizes impulsively. During a small drawdown, he panic-sold, missing recovery.
   Analysis: Emotional decisions disrupt consistency, turning profitable systems into loss-making sequences.
   Takeaway: Develop discipline, trust your plan, and maintain emotional detachment. Emotions should inform but never dictate decisions.

4. **Trader 4: Ignoring Market Context**
   Sanya relied solely on technical indicators, neglecting news and macroeconomic events. Unexpected announcements caused volatility, erasing paper profits and triggering stop-losses.

Analysis: Technical signals do not exist in isolation; ignoring market context can lead to unexpected losses.
Takeaway: Combine technical analysis with fundamental awareness. Check economic calendars, news, and market sentiment before major trades.

5. **Trader 5: Lack of Journaling and Reflection**
   Neel executed trades without documenting rationale, results, or emotional state. He repeated the same mistakes multiple times, failing to learn from experience.
   Analysis: A trading journal is essential for feedback loops, pattern recognition, and continuous improvement.
   Takeaway: Record every trade, including setup, entry, exit, outcome, and emotions. Regularly review to refine strategy and mindset.

Deeper Insights

- **Commonality of Mistakes:** Many traders fail not due to lack of skill but due to behavior and process errors.
- **Risk Management is Key:** Position sizing, stop-loss placement, and capital protection outweigh short-term profits.
- **Strategy vs. Execution:** Even perfect strategies fail if executed emotionally or without discipline.
- **Holistic Approach:** Successful trading combines technical, fundamental, and psychological awareness.
- **Continuous Learning:** Reflection, journaling, and learning from both personal and external examples accelerates improvement.

Actionable Exercise: Self-Analysis

- Take five recent trades from your demo or live account.
- Identify if any mistakes above occurred: overtrading, ignoring risk, emotional errors, lack of context, or poor journaling.
- For each mistake, note the corrective action you would apply next time.
- Develop a personal checklist to prevent repeating these errors.

Key Lesson: Learning from mistakes—both your own and others'—is more valuable than chasing quick profits. Consistency, discipline, and reflection are the cornerstones of long-term trading success.

18.4 Checklist: Mistake Prevention Pre-Trade List

Preventing mistakes starts before you even enter a trade. A structured checklist ensures discipline, reduces emotional decisions, and aligns trades with your strategy. Below is a comprehensive pre-trade checklist:

1. **Setup Verification:**
   - Is this trade based on a clearly defined strategy?
   - Does it meet your criteria for entry signals, indicators, or chart patterns?
2. **Risk Management:**
   - Maximum risk per trade: Are you adhering to the 1–2% rule?
   - Stop-loss level defined?
   - Position size calculated correctly for your account size?
3. **Reward Assessment:**
   - Is the risk-reward ratio acceptable (e.g., 1:2 or better)?
   - Target price or take-profit level defined?
4. **Market Context:**
   - Any major news, earnings, or economic releases that could affect the trade?
   - Market trend and volatility checked?
5. **Emotional Check:**
   - Are you entering this trade based on analysis, not emotions?
   - Are you calm and focused? Avoid revenge trading or FOMO-driven entries.
6. **Technical Confirmation:**

- Indicators, chart patterns, and trend lines confirm the trade?
- Confluence with multiple signals or timeframes?

7. **Log and Document:**
    - Record trade rationale, entry, stop-loss, target, and expected outcome in your journal.
    - Note any emotions or observations before entering.

8. **Execution Readiness:**
    - Broker platform set up and ready?
    - Alerts, watchlists, and dashboards configured for this trade?

Key Takeaway

Following a pre-trade checklist reduces impulsive decisions, strengthens discipline, and ensures every trade aligns with your overall trading plan. Over time, this practice improves consistency, confidence, and long-term profitability.

Key Takeaways

- Mistakes often occur due to lack of preparation, emotional bias, or ignoring risk management.
- A pre-trade checklist ensures trades are aligned with strategy, risk rules, and market conditions.
- Emotional checks and journal documentation reduce impulsive and revenge trading.
- Consistent use of checklists improves discipline, confidence, and long-term trading performance.
- Risk-reward assessment and position sizing are critical components that prevent catastrophic losses.
- Market context, technical confirmation, and execution readiness are essential before entering any trade.

Chapter 19

Advanced Tips for Long-Term Success

Introduction

Achieving consistent profits in trading is only the first step. Long-term success requires a shift in focus from individual trades to portfolio management, scaling strategies, and continuous improvement. This chapter explores techniques that professional traders use to optimize performance, reduce costs, and adapt to evolving market conditions. From technology adoption to tax planning and strategic scaling, these insights help traders move beyond short-term gains and build sustainable growth over years.

A Story: From Consistency to Growth

Priya had been trading for two years with consistent results. She realized that to move from a beginner or intermediate trader to a professional level, she needed to scale her trades, manage taxes, leverage technology, and adapt to changing markets. This chapter focuses on advanced tips to sustain long-term success.

19.1 Scaling Up Your Trading

Scaling up your trading is the process of increasing the size, frequency, or complexity of your trades as your experience, confidence, and capital grow.

While it offers the potential for larger profits, scaling also magnifies risks. Done correctly, it allows traders to compound gains systematically without exposing themselves to catastrophic losses. Done poorly, it can quickly erase your account.

Why Scaling Matters

- **Compounding Gains:** Gradually increasing your capital allocation allows profitable strategies to compound returns over time.
- **Efficiency:** A proven strategy can generate more returns when applied to larger position sizes without changing the core method.
- **Confidence Reinforcement:** Successfully scaling reinforces discipline, risk management, and psychological resilience.
- **Opportunity Maximization:** Larger capital lets you take advantage of multiple setups simultaneously or diversify across markets.

Steps to Scale Properly

1. **Confirm Strategy Consistency:** Only scale strategies with a proven positive expectancy and consistent performance over multiple trades.
2. **Increase Position Size Gradually:** Start by raising your per-trade risk or capital allocation by 10–20% at a time rather than doubling positions immediately.
3. **Maintain Risk Discipline:** Keep risk per trade within a defined percentage (commonly 1–2%) of your account size. Scaling should not mean taking reckless risks.
4. **Diversify Exposure:** Use multiple instruments, sectors, or strategies to reduce correlation risk. Avoid concentrating all your capital in a single market.
5. **Review Performance Regularly:** Keep a detailed journal noting changes in results, execution quality, emotional state, and market conditions. Adjust scaling if stress or losses increase disproportionately.

Psychological Considerations

Scaling is not just about numbers — your mind must adapt:

- **Manage Fear and Greed:** Larger positions amplify emotional pressure. Stick to your plan and avoid overtrading.
- **Discipline Under Stress:** Scaling can tempt traders to break rules. Always follow your stop-loss, take-profit, and risk parameters.
- **Comfort Zone Awareness:** Know your psychological limit. If larger trades cause anxiety or impulsive decisions, slow the scaling process.

Example

Imagine a trader with a $5,000 account risking 2% ($100) per swing trade. After 3 months of consistent profits, the account grows to $10,000. Scaling responsibly means keeping the 2% risk rule but increasing the per-trade risk to $200. The stop-loss and take-profit levels remain the same, maintaining risk control while increasing potential gains.

Common Pitfalls When Scaling

- Overconfidence, leading to oversized trades and unnecessary risk exposure.
- Ignoring subtle strategy weaknesses that appear only at higher capital levels.
- Emotional stress impacting execution, causing early exits or chasing losses.
- Lack of diversification, concentrating capital in one instrument or sector.

Pro Tips for Successful Scaling

- Scale incrementally: Increase position sizes gradually over time, reviewing each step carefully.
- Track psychological impact: Note stress levels, confidence, and decision-making quality as you scale.
- Combine scaling with other strategies: Use scaling alongside portfolio diversification, hedging, and risk management to maintain consistency.

19.2 Tax and Legal Considerations

Trading is not only about profits — it also involves understanding the legal and tax framework that governs your activities. Ignoring these aspects can lead to penalties, fines, or unnecessary losses. Being proactive about taxes and regulations ensures that you keep more of your earnings and stay compliant.

Understanding Tax Obligations

- **Capital Gains Tax:** Profits from selling stocks, crypto, or other assets may be taxed differently depending on whether they are short-term (held less than a year) or long-term (held more than a year). Short-term gains are often taxed at higher rates.
- **Dividend and Interest Income:** Earnings from dividends or interest on bonds are usually taxable in the year received. Knowing how these are reported helps you plan your tax liabilities.
- **Filing Requirements:** Keep accurate records of all trades, including dates, quantities, prices, and fees. Many countries require traders to report every transaction.

Legal Compliance

- **Regulated Brokers:** Always trade through brokers registered with appropriate financial authorities. This ensures your funds are protected and your trades are legal.
- **Insider Trading Laws:** Using non-public information to make trades is illegal and can result in severe penalties.
- **International Considerations:** If you trade across borders, understand tax treaties, withholding taxes, and reporting obligations for foreign assets.

Record Keeping and Reporting

- Maintain a detailed trading journal including buy/sell dates, quantities, prices, commissions, and net gains/losses.

- Use accounting software or spreadsheets to calculate profits and losses accurately.
- Keep receipts and statements in case of audits or disputes.

Strategic Planning

- **Tax-Loss Harvesting:** Selling losing positions to offset gains can reduce taxable income.
- **Entity Structure:** Some traders form LLCs, corporations, or partnerships to take advantage of favorable tax treatment or legal protections.
- **Professional Advice:** Consult a tax professional or financial advisor to ensure compliance and optimize strategies.

Example

Suppose a trader earns $50,000 from short-term stock trades and $10,000 from long-term investments. Short-term gains may be taxed at the individual's regular income rate, while long-term gains may enjoy a lower rate. Planning trades around tax brackets and filing deadlines can save thousands of dollars each year.

Key Takeaways

- Understand the tax treatment of all your trades — short-term, long-term, dividends, and interest.
- Trade only through regulated platforms and follow legal rules to avoid penalties.
- Keep meticulous records for accurate reporting and audits.
- Plan strategically to reduce taxes, but always stay compliant.

19.3 Leveraging Technology: AI, Bots, and Analytics

Modern trading has evolved far beyond charts and intuition. Technology offers tools to analyze vast amounts of data, automate repetitive tasks, and make more informed decisions. Leveraging AI, bots, and analytics can enhance efficiency, improve accuracy, and help traders stay competitive.

Artificial Intelligence in Trading

- **Predictive Analytics:** AI algorithms can analyze historical price data, volume, and news sentiment to predict potential price movements.
- **Pattern Recognition:** Machine learning models can detect complex chart patterns or market anomalies faster than a human eye.
- **Risk Management:** AI can simulate scenarios and stress-test portfolios to identify vulnerabilities.

Trading Bots and Automation

- **Algorithmic Execution:** Bots can execute trades automatically based on predefined rules, removing human emotion from the process.
- **High-Frequency Trading:** Bots can capitalize on tiny price discrepancies across exchanges within milliseconds.
- **Backtesting and Optimization:** Automated systems allow traders to test strategies against historical data before committing real capital.

Analytics and Visualization Tools

- **Dashboard Monitoring:** Consolidate multiple asset classes, indicators, and alerts into one interface for real-time decision-making.
- **Performance Metrics:** Analyze portfolio performance, win/loss ratios, drawdowns, and risk-adjusted returns.
- **Sentiment Analysis:** Track news, social media, and economic indicators to anticipate market shifts.

Examples

- A trader uses an AI model to identify potential breakout stocks based on historical volume patterns.
- A bot is set up to buy cryptocurrency when RSI falls below 30 and sell when it rises above 70, automating a simple momentum strategy.

- A dashboard combines stock charts, forex pairs, and crypto trends, alerting the trader when significant correlations occur.

Best Practices

- Start small: Test bots and AI models on demo accounts or low capital before scaling up.
- Monitor automation: Bots reduce human error but still require oversight to prevent unexpected losses.
- Combine human judgment with technology: AI and bots are tools, not replacements for critical thinking.

Key Takeaways

- AI, bots, and analytics provide an edge in efficiency, speed, and data processing.
- Automation reduces emotional trading but requires careful oversight.
- Combining human insight with technological tools enhances decision-making and risk management.

19.4 Adapting to Market Changes

Markets are dynamic and constantly evolving due to new technologies, economic shifts, regulations, and global events. Traders who fail to adapt risk obsolescence, while those who remain flexible can maintain profitability and reduce risk.

Understanding Market Cycles

- **Bull and Bear Phases:** Recognize the prevailing market sentiment to adjust strategies — trend-following in bullish phases and defensive approaches in bearish phases.
- **Volatility Regimes:** High-volatility periods require tighter risk controls, while low-volatility periods may favor range-bound or income-focused strategies.
- **Liquidity Shifts:** Market liquidity can change due to global events, influencing spreads, execution speed, and slippage.

Adapting Strategies

- **Diversification:** Adjust portfolio allocation across assets, sectors, or instruments depending on emerging opportunities or risks.
- **Scaling Positions:** Reduce or increase position sizes according to changing market conditions to control risk.
- **Strategy Rotation:** Employ different trading strategies (trend-following, mean-reversion, breakout) depending on market cycles and volatility.

Staying Informed

- Monitor economic calendars, earnings releases, and geopolitical events.
- Track regulatory changes that could impact trading conditions or asset accessibility.
- Use analytics tools and news feeds to spot early signs of structural shifts in markets.

Examples

- During a sudden market crash, a trader shifts from aggressive long positions to hedged or defensive assets, preserving capital.
- In a low-volatility period, a swing trader focuses on range-bound strategies rather than breakout trades.
- An algorithmic trader updates bot parameters to account for changing liquidity and volatility in cryptocurrency markets.

Best Practices

- Continuously review and update your trading plan in response to market conditions.
- Keep a flexible mindset — be ready to pause, pivot, or scale strategies as needed.
- Emphasize risk management: protecting capital is more important than forcing trades.

Key Takeaways

- Markets evolve; rigid strategies fail while flexible traders survive and thrive.
- Adaptation involves strategy, position sizing, and informed decision-making.
- Staying aware, prepared, and disciplined ensures resilience in dynamic markets.

Exercise: 6-Month Progress Review & Adjustment Plan

This exercise helps you reflect on your trading journey, evaluate performance, and make adjustments to improve results over the next six months. Consistent review and iteration are key to long-term success.

Step 1: Collect Your Trading Data

- Gather all trade logs, including entry and exit points, position sizes, stop-loss and take-profit levels.
- Record all relevant indicators, market conditions, and notes on why trades were executed.
- Include emotional observations: what feelings influenced your decisions, if any.

Step 2: Analyze Performance Metrics

- Calculate key metrics:
  - Win rate (% of profitable trades)
  - Average risk-to-reward ratio
  - Maximum drawdown
  - Total profit/loss over 6 months
- Identify which strategies, instruments, or timeframes performed best.
- Spot recurring mistakes or emotional traps that led to losses.

Step 3: Set Goals and Adjustments

- Define realistic goals for the next 6 months:
  - Example: Increase win rate from 55% to 60%
  - Example: Reduce average drawdown from 10% to 5%
- Adjust your trading plan based on insights:
  - Focus more on profitable strategies or instruments
  - Modify position sizing rules
  - Implement better risk controls

Step 4: Emotional and Discipline Check

- Reflect on how emotions affected trades.
- Plan steps to improve discipline:
  - Use journaling to track feelings before and after trades
  - Set strict rules for trade execution and risk management
  - Schedule review sessions regularly

Step 5: Document the Plan

- Create a written 6-month action plan:
  - Strategies to focus on
  - Risk management rules
  - Goals and performance targets
  - Schedule for review and adjustment
- Treat this as a dynamic document — update as market conditions and skills evolve.

Outcome

By completing this exercise, you gain:

- Clear visibility into strengths, weaknesses, and trading patterns
- A structured roadmap for improvement
- A disciplined, probabilistic approach to decision-making

Key Takeaways

- Regular performance review is essential for long-term trading success.
- Tracking both quantitative metrics (win rate, risk-reward, drawdowns) and qualitative observations (emotions, discipline) provides a complete picture.
- Adjusting your trading plan based on real data helps refine strategies, manage risk, and improve profitability.
- Setting realistic goals for the next period ensures continuous improvement without overtrading or emotional decisions.
- Documentation of strategies, rules, and progress promotes accountability and supports disciplined trading habits.
- Treat your trading plan as a dynamic, evolving roadmap that adapts to changes in markets, personal skill, and risk tolerance.

Part VII

Mastering the Probabilistic Mindset

Chapter 20

Core Lessons from the Book

Introduction

After exploring markets, strategies, tools, and psychology, it's time to step back and see the bigger picture. This chapter consolidates the essential lessons from the book — the principles, habits, and mindset that separate consistent traders and investors from those who struggle. Understanding these core concepts helps you make probabilistic decisions, manage risk effectively, and approach financial markets with clarity and discipline.

A Story: From Chaos to Clarity

Aarav started his trading journey full of excitement but little direction. He jumped from one strategy to another, chased trends, and let emotions dictate his trades. Over time, he realized that success wasn't about finding a "secret formula" but about mastering the fundamentals: risk management, discipline, proper planning, and continuous learning. By applying these core lessons consistently, Aarav moved from chaotic trades to a structured, confident, and profitable approach.

20.1 The Probabilistic Mindset for Life Decisions

In trading, success rarely comes from certainty; it comes from understanding probabilities, managing risk, and making decisions with favorable expected outcomes. The same principle applies to life: every choice, from career moves to personal decisions, carries probabilities and potential consequences. Thinking probabilistically allows you to make rational decisions, reduce biases, and improve long-term outcomes.

Core Principles

- **Think in Probabilities, Not Certainties:** Life is uncertain. Avoid expecting only one outcome. Instead, assign probabilities to different possibilities and plan accordingly.
- **Assess Risk vs. Reward:** Consider both the potential upside and downside of each decision. High-probability, low-risk choices compound over time and lead to more consistent success.
- **Expected Value (EV) Analysis:** Decisions can be quantified using expected value:

  $$EV = (ProbabilityofSuccess \times Reward) - (ProbabilityofFailure \times Loss)$$

  Using EV helps turn subjective guesses into structured, rational thinking.
- **Account for Uncertainty:** Always assume that rare events can occur. Adjust probabilities and strategies based on historical data and trends, but remain flexible.
- **Learn from Feedback:** Continuously update your assessments based on outcomes. Probabilistic thinking is dynamic — probabilities evolve as new information becomes available.

Illustrative Example: Career Choice

Imagine choosing between two job offers:

- Job A: 70% chance of high growth (\$50,000 increase in 5 years), 30% chance of stagnation (\$0 increase)

- Job B: 50% chance of high growth ($80,000), 50% chance of stagnation ($0)

Calculate expected value:

$$EV_A = (0.7 \times 50,000) + (0.3 \times 0) = 35,000$$

$$EV_B = (0.5 \times 80,000) + (0.5 \times 0) = 40,000$$

Although Job B has higher uncertainty, the expected value is higher. A probabilistic mindset helps you choose rationally rather than emotionally.

Example: Personal Finance Decision

Suppose you are deciding whether to invest in a startup:

- 30% chance to double your investment ($20,000 gain)
- 50% chance to break even ($0 gain)
- 20% chance to lose your investment ($10,000 loss)

$$EV = (0.3 \times 20,000) + (0.5 \times 0) + (0.2 \times -10,000) = 6,000 - 2,000 = 4,000$$

Even with risk, the positive expected value indicates this is statistically a good decision if you can tolerate the downside.

Practical Life Applications

- **Career Decisions:** Evaluate potential outcomes, growth opportunities, and risks. Make incremental bets aligned with your long-term goals.
- **Investments:** Analyze risk-reward ratios, probabilities of success, and portfolio diversification using expected value.
- **Health and Lifestyle Choices:** Consider probabilistic outcomes of decisions, such as exercise habits, diet, or preventive measures.
- **Time Management:** Allocate effort toward high-probability tasks that provide the greatest return on your time and energy.
- **Emotional Decisions:** Reduce biases like overconfidence, fear, and loss aversion by framing choices probabilistically rather than absolutely.

A Story: Applying Probabilistic Thinking

Riya wanted to start investing but was unsure which assets to choose. Instead of guessing, she listed three options with potential outcomes and probabilities:

- Stock A: 60% chance to gain $10,000, 40% chance to lose $5,000
- Stock B: 50% chance to gain $15,000, 50% chance to lose $10,000
- Index Fund: 80% chance to gain $6,000, 20% chance to lose $1,000

Calculating expected values:

$$EV_A = (0.6 \times 10,000) - (0.4 \times 5,000) = 6,000 - 2,000 = 4,000$$

$$EV_B = (0.5 \times 15,000) - (0.5 \times 10,000) = 7,500 - 5,000 = 2,500$$

$$EV_{Index} = (0.8 \times 6,000) - (0.2 \times 1,000) = 4,800 - 200 = 4,600$$

Riya realized the Index Fund had the best risk-adjusted outcome. She allocated most of her capital there and took smaller positions in Stocks A and B, achieving consistent growth while managing risk.

Key Takeaways

- Life, like trading, is uncertain. Decisions should be made with probabilities in mind.
- Expected value helps quantify risk and reward for rational decision-making.
- Small, consistent positive EV decisions compound into long-term success.
- Probabilistic thinking reduces emotional bias and improves resilience in uncertain situations.
- Continuously update your assumptions as new data emerges, making your decisions dynamic and adaptive.

20.2 Building Multi-Generational Wealth

Wealth is not just about personal financial freedom — it can be a tool to empower future generations. Building multi-generational wealth means creating strategies, habits, and structures that allow your family to benefit financially long after your lifetime.

Core Principles

- **Start Early and Leverage Compounding:** The earlier you begin investing and saving, the more time your money has to grow exponentially. Compound interest turns small, consistent contributions into significant wealth over decades.
- **Diversification Across Asset Classes:** Spread wealth across stocks, bonds, real estate, businesses, and alternative assets. Diversification reduces risk and stabilizes long-term growth.
- **Risk Management:** Protect capital using insurance, hedging, and conservative allocation strategies. Preserving wealth is as important as growing it.
- **Education and Financial Literacy:** Teach children and heirs the principles of investing, saving, and risk. Knowledge is a transferable asset that sustains wealth across generations.
- **Estate Planning and Legal Structures:** Use trusts, wills, and family offices to ensure that wealth is passed efficiently and according to your wishes, minimizing taxes and disputes.
- **Philanthropy and Purpose:** Allocate a portion of wealth to social impact or charitable initiatives. Giving back can instill values and purpose in the next generation.

Illustrative Example

Consider a family that invests $50,000 annually with an average return of 7%:

- Over 30 years, this grows to approximately $4.5 million.
- If the next generation continues the same strategy, compounding could create over $12 million across two generations.

Key Strategies

1. **Long-Term Investing:** Focus on assets with growth potential over decades rather than short-term speculation.

2. **Dividend and Passive Income:** Reinvest dividends or rental income to grow capital without constant intervention.

3. **Regular Review and Adaptation:** Markets, tax laws, and family circumstances change. Periodically review investments and legal structures.

4. **Teach Financial Discipline:** Instill habits like budgeting, saving, and rational decision-making in younger generations.

5. **Leverage Professional Guidance:** Wealth managers, estate planners, and tax advisors help implement strategies efficiently.

A Story: Passing Down Wealth Wisely

Anand, a successful entrepreneur, built a profitable business over 25 years. Rather than just leaving his assets to his children, he created a family trust, invested in diversified portfolios, and educated his children about money management. By the time Anand retired, his family had financial security and a roadmap to grow wealth responsibly, ensuring multi-generational prosperity.

Key Takeaways

- Start early and let compounding work in your favor.

- Diversify across assets and protect capital with risk management strategies.

- Educate heirs on financial literacy to sustain wealth beyond your lifetime.

- Use legal structures and estate planning to preserve and efficiently transfer assets.

- Multi-generational wealth is a combination of capital growth, knowledge, discipline, and purposeful planning.

20.3 The Future of Trading & AI

The trading world is rapidly evolving, driven by technological innovation, big data, and artificial intelligence (AI). Understanding these trends is essential for both new and experienced traders who wish to stay ahead in the modern markets.

1. AI-Powered Trading

AI and machine learning models analyze vast datasets to identify patterns and predict market movements. Unlike humans, AI can process information 24/7, learning from past trades, news, and alternative data sources.

- **Algorithmic Trading:** AI can automatically execute trades based on pre-defined conditions, reducing emotional bias.
- **Predictive Analytics:** Machine learning models forecast trends and price movements using historical and real-time data.
- **Risk Management:** AI can dynamically adjust portfolio risk levels by analyzing volatility, correlations, and market sentiment.

2. Big Data and Alternative Data Sources

Modern traders have access to vast amounts of information beyond traditional financial reports:

- Social media sentiment and news analytics.
- Satellite imagery to track production or retail activity.
- Web scraping for market trends and consumer behavior.

AI leverages this data to create actionable insights that were previously impossible to obtain manually.

3. Automation and Smart Execution

Automation allows for faster trade execution, efficient order routing, and reduced human error. High-frequency trading (HFT) and AI-powered bots can respond to market changes in milliseconds, giving institutional traders a competitive edge.

However, retail traders can also benefit from semi-automated strategies, such as:

- Pre-set alerts for buy/sell conditions.
- AI-assisted portfolio rebalancing.
- Risk scenario simulations using predictive models.

4. Democratization of Trading Technology

AI and advanced analytics are no longer limited to hedge funds and large institutions. Retail platforms now provide:

- Algorithmic trading templates and strategy builders.
- AI-driven stock screeners and signal generators.
- Visual dashboards that simplify complex market data.

This democratization allows individual traders to compete more effectively while learning sophisticated methods.

5. Challenges and Considerations

While AI offers significant advantages, it also introduces new risks:

- Overreliance on algorithms may reduce human judgment.
- Models can fail during unprecedented market conditions.
- Ethical and regulatory issues around AI-driven trading are still evolving.

6. Looking Ahead

The future of trading will likely blend human intuition with AI-driven insights:

- Traders will focus on strategy design, risk oversight, and decision-making.
- AI will handle data analysis, pattern recognition, and execution.
- Continuous learning and adaptation will remain crucial as markets and technologies evolve.

Key Takeaways

- AI is transforming trading through predictive analytics, automation, and risk management.
- Access to big data and alternative datasets enhances trading insights.
- Retail traders can leverage AI tools but should combine them with human judgment.
- Ethical, regulatory, and model risks must be understood and managed.
- The most successful traders will blend technology with strategy, discipline, and adaptability.

20.4 Checklist: The Probabilistic Investor's Toolkit

A probabilistic investor approaches trading and investing by thinking in terms of odds, expected value, and risk-reward balance. This toolkit provides a structured checklist to help make disciplined, informed, and data-driven decisions.

1. Define Your Probabilities

- Estimate the likelihood of different outcomes for each trade or investment.
- Consider historical data, market conditions, and fundamental/technical indicators.
- Example: A swing trade may have a 60% chance to gain $200 and a 40% chance to lose $100.

2. Calculate Expected Value (EV)

- Use the formula:

$$EV = (Gp \times PotentialGain) + (Lp \times PotentialLoss)$$

Where Gp = Probability of Gain Lp = Probability of Loss

- Only take trades or investments with positive expected value over the long term.
- Example: Using the previous probabilities, $EV = (0.6 \times 200) + (0.4 \times -100) = 120 - 40 = 80$. Positive EV indicates a favorable trade.

3. Assess Risk-Reward Ratio

- Determine how much you are risking relative to potential reward.
- Favor trades where the potential reward exceeds the risk.
- Example: Risking $100 to potentially gain $200 yields a 2:1 reward-to-risk ratio.

4. Position Sizing and Capital Allocation

- Allocate a fraction of your total capital based on risk tolerance.
- Common rule: risk 1–2% of your capital per trade to manage drawdowns.
- Adjust position sizes according to confidence level and expected value.

5. Define Entry, Exit, and Stop Criteria

- Set clear rules for when to enter, take profits, or cut losses.
- Avoid emotional decisions by predefining conditions based on probabilities and risk-reward.
- Example: Enter a trade only when indicators align and exit if the price moves against you by a predetermined amount.

6. Track and Review Performance

- Maintain a trading journal with outcomes, probabilities, and decisions.
- Review trades periodically to refine probability estimates and improve decision-making.
- Identify recurring mistakes and adjust your toolkit accordingly.

7. Continuous Learning

- Stay updated on market changes, new tools, and analytical techniques.
- Use feedback from real trades to improve probability assessments and risk management strategies.

Key Takeaways

- Always think in terms of probabilities and expected value.
- Predefine risk, reward, and position sizing before entering trades.
- Track results and learn from outcomes systematically.
- The probabilistic mindset reduces emotional decision-making and improves long-term profitability.

Key Takeaways

- A probabilistic mindset improves decision-making by focusing on odds, expected value, and risk-reward balance.
- Always define probabilities and calculate expected value before taking trades or investments.
- Maintain disciplined position sizing and capital allocation to protect your portfolio.
- Predefine entry, exit, and stop-loss criteria to minimize emotional decisions.
- Track and review performance systematically to refine strategies and improve accuracy.
- Continuous learning and adapting to market changes are essential for long-term success.
- Using a structured toolkit ensures consistency, reduces mistakes, and maximizes probabilistic edge in investing.

Extras

Glossary

This glossary provides definitions of key trading, investing, and financial terms for quick reference.

- **Ask:** The lowest price at which a seller is willing to sell a security or asset.
- **Bid:** The highest price at which a buyer is willing to purchase a security or asset.
- **Spread:** The difference between the bid and ask prices of an asset.
- **Leverage:** Using borrowed capital to increase potential returns on an investment, which also increases potential risk.
- **Margin:** The amount of capital required to open and maintain a leveraged position.
- **Stop Loss:** An order placed to sell an asset automatically when it reaches a certain price to limit potential losses.
- **Take Profit (Target):** An order to automatically close a trade when it reaches a predetermined profit level.
- **Candlestick:** A chart element representing price movement in a given period, showing the open, high, low, and close prices.
- **Line Chart:** A chart connecting closing prices over time to show general price trends.
- **Bar Chart:** A chart showing open, high, low, and close prices for each period as vertical bars.
- **Moving Average (MA):** A technical indicator that smooths out price data by averaging it over a specific period (e.g., SMA, EMA).

- **RSI (Relative Strength Index):** A momentum oscillator measuring the speed and change of price movements, indicating overbought or oversold conditions.
- **MACD (Moving Average Convergence Divergence):** A trend-following momentum indicator that shows the relationship between two moving averages of a security's price.
- **Bollinger Bands:** A volatility indicator that consists of a moving average and two standard deviation lines above and below it.
- **Support:** A price level where buying interest is strong enough to prevent the price from falling further.
- **Resistance:** A price level where selling pressure is strong enough to prevent the price from rising further.
- **Trend Line:** A straight line drawn on a chart to indicate the general direction of the market or security.
- **Breakout:** When price moves above resistance or below support, often signaling a new trend.
- **Swing Trading:** A medium-term trading strategy that seeks to capture price swings over days or weeks.
- **Day Trading:** Buying and selling financial instruments within the same trading day.
- **Position Trading:** A longer-term strategy where trades are held for weeks to months based on trend analysis.
- **Options:** Financial derivatives that give the holder the right, but not the obligation, to buy (call) or sell (put) an asset at a predetermined price.
- **Call Option:** A contract giving the buyer the right to purchase an asset at a specified price before expiration.
- **Put Option:** A contract giving the buyer the right to sell an asset at a specified price before expiration.
- **Arbitrage:** Simultaneous buying and selling of an asset in different markets to profit from price discrepancies.

- **Hedging:** Using financial instruments to reduce or eliminate the risk of adverse price movements.
- **Volatility:** The degree of variation in a financial instrument's price over time.
- **Liquidity:** How easily an asset can be bought or sold without affecting its price.
- **Fundamental Analysis:** Evaluating a security by analyzing financial statements, economic indicators, and other qualitative and quantitative factors.
- **Technical Analysis:** Analyzing price charts and indicators to predict future market movements based on historical patterns.
- **Risk Management:** Techniques used to limit financial losses and protect capital, including position sizing, stop-loss placement, and diversification.
- **Expected Value (EV):** The average outcome of a trade or investment when probabilities of gains and losses are considered.
- **Probabilistic Thinking:** Evaluating potential outcomes in terms of likelihood and impact rather than certainty.
- **Portfolio Diversification:** Spreading investments across various assets to reduce overall risk.
- **Execution:** The process of completing a trade order in the market.
- **Broker:** An intermediary that facilitates buying and selling of financial instruments on behalf of traders.
- **Exchange:** A regulated marketplace where financial instruments are traded.

This glossary can be expanded as you progress, including new terms, tools, and strategies you encounter in trading and investing.

Recommended Books, Courses, and Resources

Books

Technical Analysis and Trading:

- *Technical Analysis of the Financial Markets* — John J. Murphy
- *Japanese Candlestick Charting Techniques* — Steve Nison
- *Encyclopedia of Chart Patterns* — Thomas Bulkowski
- *Trading for a Living* — Dr. Alexander Elder
- *The New Trading for a Living* — Dr. Alexander Elder
- *Technical Analysis Using Multiple Timeframes* — Brian Shannon
- *Market Wizards* series — Jack D. Schwager

Options, Derivatives, and Quantitative Trading:

- *Option Volatility & Pricing* — Sheldon Natenberg
- *The Volatility Edge in Options Trading* — Jeff Augen
- *Algorithmic Trading* — Ernest P. Chan
- *Quantitative Trading* — Ernest P. Chan
- *Advances in Financial Machine Learning* — Marcos López de Prado
- *Trading Systems and Methods* — Perry J. Kaufman

Investing and Value:

- *The Intelligent Investor* — Benjamin Graham
- *One Up on Wall Street* — Peter Lynch
- *Common Stocks and Uncommon Profits* — Philip Fisher
- *The Little Book That Still Beats the Market* — Joel Greenblatt
- *Margin of Safety* — Seth Klarman

Risk, Probabilities, and Trading Psychology:

- *Fooled by Randomness* — Nassim Taleb
- *The Black Swan* — Nassim Taleb
- *The Art of Thinking in Probabilities* — King
- *Trading in the Zone* — Mark Douglas
- *The Disciplined Trader* — Mark Douglas

Courses and Online Learning

Foundations:

- Coursera: *Financial Markets* — Yale University
- Khan Academy: *Finance & Capital Markets*
- Investopedia Academy: Beginner courses

Applied Trading:

- CME Group: Futures and options tutorials
- Udemy: Stock, Forex, and Crypto trading courses
- QuantInsti: EPAT – Algorithmic and Quantitative Trading
- Trading Academy: Technical and fundamental trading strategies

Advanced / Quantitative:

- Coursera: *Machine Learning for Trading* — Georgia Tech
- MIT OpenCourseWare: Financial Engineering
- QuantStart: Algorithmic trading tutorials
- Interactive Brokers Traders' Academy: Advanced trading tools

Websites and Tools

- Market Data: Yahoo Finance, Google Finance, MacroTrends
- Economic Data: FRED, Trading Economics
- Trading Platforms: TradingView, Thinkorswim, MT4/MT5, NinjaTrader
- Crypto: CoinMarketCap, CoinGecko, Binance Academy
- News & Sentiment: Bloomberg, Reuters, CNBC, Seeking Alpha

Tips for Using Resources

- Start with foundational books and courses before moving to advanced topics.
- Use demo accounts or paper trading to practice before risking capital.
- Participate in communities for mentorship, discussion, and updates.
- Keep revisiting books, courses, and tools as your trading skills evolve.

Useful Tools, Websites, and Apps

Trading Platforms

- **MetaTrader 4 / 5 (MT4/MT5):** Widely used for forex and CFD trading, supports technical analysis, automated trading, and backtesting.
- **TradingView:** Web-based charting platform with advanced tools, community ideas, and alerts for stocks, forex, crypto, and more.
- **Thinkorswim (by TD Ameritrade):** Comprehensive platform for stocks, options, futures, and forex with advanced analysis and paper trading.
- **Interactive Brokers:** Global brokerage with professional trading tools, low fees, and multi-asset access.

Market Data and Research Tools

- **Yahoo Finance / Google Finance:** Free real-time stock quotes, historical data, news, and charts.
- **Investing.com:** Global financial data, economic calendars, news, and analysis.
- **Finviz:** Stock screeners, heatmaps, and market analysis tools.
- **Morningstar:** In-depth analysis for stocks, mutual funds, and ETFs.

Economic Indicators and News

- **Trading Economics:** Global economic data, forecasts, and charts.
- **Bloomberg / Reuters:** News, analysis, and market-moving events.
- **Eikon / Refinitiv:** Professional financial data and news platforms.

Portfolio Tracking and Management

- **Excel / Google Sheets:** Custom portfolio tracking and trade analysis.
- **Personal Capital / Mint:** Track investments, net worth, and asset allocation.
- **Sharesight:** Automated portfolio tracking, dividends, and performance reporting.

Education and Backtesting Tools

- **Coursera / Udemy / Skillshare:** Courses on trading, investing, and technical analysis.
- **QuantConnect / AlgoTrader:** Platforms for backtesting and algorithmic trading.
- **ThinkScript / Pine Script:** Scripting tools for custom indicators and automated strategies.

Community and Forums

- **Reddit:** Subreddits like r/StockMarket, r/Forex, r/CryptoCurrency for discussion and ideas.
- **Stack Exchange:** Quantitative Finance
- **Meetup.com** : Local trading and investing meetups
- **TradingView Community Ideas:** Follow active traders and ideas.
- **Discord / Telegram Groups:** Focused trading communities and mentorship channels.

Journal Template

Checklist

Date		Analysis Done? (Y/N)	
Events/News		Risk ≤ 2%? (Y/N/Other)	
Market Conditions / Key Levels		Market Context Favorable? (Y/N)	
Plan/Strategy		Emotional State OK? (Y/N)	

Trade Entries

Time	Symbol	Trade Type	Trade Setup & Quality (1–5)	Probability (%)	Size / Price	SL / TP	Expected R:R	Notes

Trade Exits

Time	Symbol	Exit Reason	P/L ($ / %)	Win/Loss	SL Hit?	TP Hit?	Deviation from Plan?	Actual R:R	Notes

Post-Trade Analysis

Followed Plan? (Y/N)	Position Sizing / Risk ≤ 2%? (Y/N/Other)	Market Context Favorable? (Y/N/Other)	Emotional Discipline OK?	Exit logical (not emotional)?	Mistakes / Improvement Notes

Notes

Profit ($)	
Gain (%)	
Average R:R	
Average Win Rate (%)	

www.ingramcontent.com/pod-product-compliance
Lightning Source LLC
Chambersburg PA
CBHW050524240926
51846CB00003B/684
9789334430370